Making CUSHIONS & PILLOWS

NINA GRANLUND SÆTHER

D&C
David and Charles

www.stitchcraftcreate.co.uk

CONTENTS

FOREWORD

Give your sofa the wow-factor by decorating it with unique handmade cushions and pillows.

New cushions and pillows are always fun! They liven up your décor and can completely change the impression of a room. Even better than a store bought pillow is one that you have made yourself – the one you have struggled with that shows small signs of being homemade, the one that almost nobody has a copy of – it will be the icing on the cake for your couch.

Needlework is rarely seen as value-added. Some like the fact that we amuse ourselves with knitting and crochet needles in front of the tv! Others laugh at the complicated and time-consuming techniques and wonder why somebody would want to spend time, effort and money on making clothes and other artefacts when most of it can be bought much cheaper in a store.

Nevertheless, there is a knitting wave going through the country. Hooray for that! Handmade is again relevant. There are loads of pretty yarns available and the knitting needles are clinking. Some prefer the crochet hook, while others have discovered needles and embroidery yarn. Some desire traditional patterns, while others are inspired by new designs. Hundreds of needlework blogs online testify swarming activity and provoke further creativity. It makes an old needlework enthusiast very happy!

I hope that you will be inspired to continue using the needlework techniques that have been passed down the generations and are still so applicable today, translated into current styles that will brighten up your home. I believe the trend for interior design and decorating, reflected in the hundreds of decorating blogs online, will encourage people to want to make unique pieces for themselves, which can be done with a little help from the projects in this book. Pillows and cushions are so easy to make and you can have fun experimenting with a wealth of different fabrics and styles – only your imagination will set the limits on what you can achieve.

Nina Granlund Sæther

Knitting abbreviations
st stitch
k knit
ktog knit together
p purl
ptog purl together
CO cast on
sl1 slip one stitch
psso pass slipped stitch over
cn cable needle
tk twisted knit
yo yarn over needle

Crochet abbreviations
ch chain stitch
sc single crochet
sl st slip stitch
dc double crochet

Unless otherwise noted, use a seam allowance of 1cm (⅜in). Pillows and cushions are available in different sizes and qualities. Usually they are filled with feathers or down, or with synthetic filling. It is also possible to make the pillows and cushions yourself and fill them with, for example, carded wool. The pillows in this book are bought in various stores; both local boutiques and large chains. Some are also handmade. I recommend washing and ironing all linen and cotton fabrics used for backs, before use – this will prevent them from shrinking.

NATURALLY

RENOVATION ADDICTION AND CUSHION FEVER

Renovation addiction is a contagious disease that mainly affects women between the ages of 20 and 40 years old. The disease blooms in the autumn along with other viral diseases, and attacks the parts of the brain that process impressions. At worst, the disease can be chronic and you must live with it for the rest of your life. Treatment of the disease is very difficult, and in some cases, impossible.

The source of infection is usually friends who are renovating, but the virus can also be transmitted through the optic nerves by reading magazines or blogs and seeing how others do things. It is estimated that people who are open to new impulses and ideas are more easily infected than others – that is, people who are original, imaginative, creative, curious and insightful.

Cushion fever is a mild form of renovation addiction, as it is mainly the sofa that the infected wants to freshen up. The sources of infection are the same as described above. He or she gets an immediate urge to throw away worn and unfashionable cushions and replace them with those that are trendier.

There is not always a great understanding of the nature of this disease from potential partners and spouses, as tables and chairs are easily filled with ongoing projects. Needles, yarn and threads can be scattered around for days – sometimes weeks. Chores such as cleaning and dusting are then ignored.

Dazzling diamonds

Materials
Zip 35cm (13¾in)

Yarn
Mitu from Rauma Ullvarefabrikk (alpaca/wool) 250g (8¾oz) in sheep white no. 0010

3.5mm (size 4) needles

Finished size: 50 x 50cm (20 x 20in)

CO 184cm (72½in) on a circular needle and knit in the round.
Front: Start with k4, p2, k10, p2, DIAMOND PATTERN, and finish with k1, p2, k10, p2, k4. The pattern measures 103cm (40½in) altogether.
Back: Knit k the whole time. Amount of k on the back is only 81cm (32in). This is because of the cable pattern in the front that contracts and shrinks.

Diamond pattern:
CR means cross right: place 1 st on cn behind the work, k1 from left needle and then k1 from cn (4 CR means to repeat CR 4 times.)

CL means cross left: Place 1 st on cn in front of the work, knit k1 from left needle and then k1 from cn.

Row 1: *K1, CL1, CR4, k1, CL4, CR1*.
Repeat from * to * 3 times (total 22 sts, 3 times is 66 sts).
Row 2: And all other even rows: k.
Row 3: *K2, CL1, CR3, k3, CL3, CR1, k1*. Repeat from * to * 3 times.

Row 5: *K1, CL2, CR3, k1, CL3, CR2*.
Repeat from * to * 3 times.
Row 7: *K2, CL2, CR2, k3, CL2, CR2, k1*. Repeat from * to * 3 times.
Row 9: *K1, CL3, CR2, k1, CL2, CR3*.
Repeat from * to * 3 times.
Row 11: *K2, CL3, CR1, k3, CL1, CR3, k1*. Repeat from * to * 3 times.
Row 13: *K1, CL4, CR1, k1, CL1, CR4*.
Repeat from * to * 3 times.
Row 15: *K2, CL4, k3, CR4, k4*.
Repeat from * to * 3 times.
** See NB on next page.
Row 17: *K1, CL5, k1, CR5*.
Repeat from * to * 3 times.
Row 19: *K1, CR5, k1, CL5*.
Repeat from * to * 3 times.
(Now the pattern is reversed and goes in the opposite direction.)
Row 21: *K2, CR4, k3, CL4, k1*.
Repeat from * to * 3 times.
Row 23: *K1, CR4, CL1, k1, CR1, CL4*.
Repeat from * to * 3 times.
Row 25: *K2, CR3, CL1, k3, CR1, CL3, k1*. Repeat from * to * 3 times.
Row 27: *K1, CR3, CL2, k1, CR2, CL3*.
Repeat from * to * 3 times.
Row 29: *K2, CR2, CL2, k3, CR2, CL2, k1*. Repeat from * to * 3 times.
Row 31: *K1, CR2, CL3, k1, CR3, CL2*.
Repeat from * to * 3 times.
Row 33: *K2, CR1, CL3, k3, CR3, CL1, k1*. Repeat from * to * 3 times.
Row 35: *K1, CR1, CL4, k1, CR4, CL1*.
Repeat from * to * 3 times.
Row 36: Knit k.

NB: When you have knitted row 16, turn the cables on the side the first time. Do this by placing the first 5 sts on a cn behind the work, knit the next 5 before you knit k on cn. Turn the cables every 8 rows. Use a safety pin or similar to keep track of the rows. The cables are turned 11 times in total. The diamond pattern from row 1 to row 36 is repeated 3 times. Cast (bind) off.

Assembly:
Press the work gently. Sew in the zip as described in Good Advice. Sew the sides on the bottom and top with mattress stitch. The bubble edges are made by sewing overstitch with double thread around the 3 outermost sts on each side. Cast the stitch around 3 sts. Tighten gently to achieve the bubble effect.

Star gazing

Materials
Zip 30cm (12in)

Yarn
Hubro from Dale Garn (wool)
200g (7oz) sheep white no. 0020

9mm (size 13) needles

Finished size: 45 x 45cm (17¾ x 17¾in)

Front:
CO 49 sts. Start with moss stitch. Begin with the bottom row and read the pattern from right to left. White squares indicate k and black squares indicate p. Work back the next row. Now the pattern needs to be read from left to right, white squares indicate p and black squares indicate k. The work should measure 14cm (5½in) when you begin with the star.

Continue back and forth until the work is complete. Cast (bind) off while you knit the last row in the pattern.

The back is made the same way as the front.

Assembly:
Iron (press) the two pieces carefully. Insert a 30cm (12in) long zip by hand (see Good Advice). Then place the two pieces wrong side to wrong side and sew around using buttonhole stitches in the same yarn as used for the cushion.

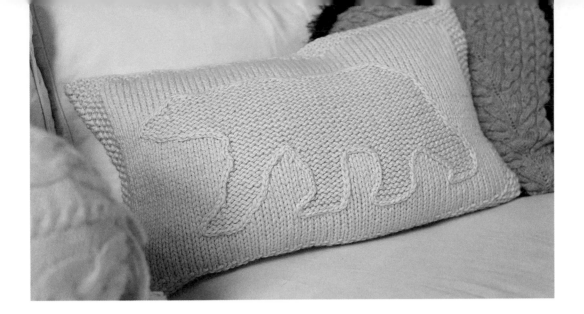

Polar bear

Materials
Zip 50cm (20in)

Yarn
Hubro from Dalene Garn (wool)
250g (8¾oz) sheep white no. 0020

9mm (size 13) needles

Finished size: 40 x 60cm (16 x 24in)

Front:
CO 70 sts. Start with moss stitch as shown in the diagram. Begin with the bottom row and read the pattern from right to left. White squares indicate k and black squares indicate p. Work back the next row. Now the pattern needs to be read from left to right, white squares indicate p and black squares indicate k.

Continue back and forth until the work is complete. Cast (bind) off while knitting the last row in the diagram.

The back is knitted the same as the front, polar bear optional.

Assembly:
To highlight the image, sew a seam around the polar bear with chain stitch. Start in the middle of the back and follow the purl stitches around the bear. Iron (press) the two pieces carefully. Insert a zip by hand (see Good Advice). Then place the two pieces wrong side to wrong side and sew around using buttonhole or overstitch stitches in the same yarn as used for the cushion.

This cushion is not difficult to make, even though it looks complicated. Simply start at the bottom tip and CO on each side of the central stitch. The work will look a little odd and stretched when it is complete, however to make a nice heart shape it is important to follow the instructions on blocking in Good Advice.

Cable heart cushion

Materials

Back: Grey wool fabric: 60 x 45cm (18 x 24in). You can also knit another heart to use for the back.

Yarn

Falk from Dale Garn (wool)
150g (5¼oz) grey no. 0004
Plippi from Rauma Ullvarefabrikk (alpaca/nylon)
50g (1¾oz) grey
Beo from Larartus (polyamide)
50g (1¾oz) black

3.5mm (size 4) and 9mm (size 13) needles

Front:
Row 1: CO 7 sts with 3.5mm (size 4) needles.
Row 2: K2, p3 and k2.
Row 3: P2, k1, CO 1 st on each side of the central stitch, k1 and p2.
Row 4: K2, p5 and k2.
Row 5: P2, k2, CO 1 st on each side of the central stitch, k2 and p2.
Row 6: K2, p7 and k2.
Row 7: P2, k3, CO 1 st on each side of the central stitch, k3 and p2.

Row 8: K2, p9 and k2.
Row 9: P2, k4, M1 st on each side of the central stitch, k4 and p2.
Row 10: K2, p11 and k2.
Row 11: P2, k5, M1 st on each side of the central stitch, k5 p2.
Row 12: K2, p13 and k2.
Row 13: P2, k6, M1 st on each side of the central stitch, k6 and p2.
Row 14: K2, p15 and k2.
Row 15: P2, k7, M1 st on each side of the central stitch, k7 and p2.
Row 16: K2, p8, k1, p8 and k2.
Row 17: P2, k8, M1 p st on each side of the central stitch, k8 and p2.
Row 18: K2, p8, k3, p8 and k2.
Row 19: P2, place the next 4 sts on a cn behind the work, knit 4 sts, then knit the 4 from the cn (1 right cable), p1, M p1 st on each side of the central stitch, p1, place the next 4 on a cn in front of the work, knit 4 sts, then knit the 4 sts from the cn (left cable), p2.
Row 20: K2, p8, k5, p8 and k2.

Continue the same way by M1 st on each side of the central stitch every other needle as well as continuing the cables. This means that you have to turn when you are at row 9 and 19.

Repeat until you have 165 sts on the needle.
Next row: K82sts, cast off 1sts, knit to end. Now you should have 82 sts on each

side. Leave the sts on the right side alone
while you continue on the left side.
*Begin by knitting p2 and the two next sts k to 1,
knit to the end of the needle. Do the same thing
back; k2, the next 2 sts ptog to 1, knit to the end
of the needle. Knit back and forth without casting
(binding) off*. Repeat from * to * 4 times.
Continue knitting cables and turning as before.
*Knit p2, knit the next 2 sts k joined as 1, knit to
the end of the needle. Do the same thing back:
k2, the next 2 sts p joined as 1, knit to the end
of the needle*. Repeat from * to * 4 times.
Cast (bind) off the 3 first sts, knit to the end
of the needle. Do the same thing back.
*Cast (bind) off the first 5 sts, knit to the
end of the needle. Do the same thing
back*. Repeat from * to * 5 times.
Cast (bind) off the last 10 sts.
Knit the right side of the work in the same way.

Fur trim:
CO 5 sts with 1 grey and 1 black yarn on 9mm
(size 13) needles. Knit k back and forth with
double thread until it measures 175cm (69in).
Cast (bind) off and attach thread.

Assembly:
Sew in all loose threads on the work.

Sketch and cut out a heart that measures about
60cm (24in) in height and about 45cm (18in) in
width. Place the drawing on a porous board,
and attach the work (see Good Advice).

Use the same pattern to cut out a
back piece in grey wool fabric.

Place the knitted heart and the back piece wrong
side to wrong side and sew together. Leave an
opening of about 10cm (4in) on one side. Fill
the pillow with washed and carded wool or
use a foam cushion insert. Sew together.

Hide the stitched edges with the fur trim. Sew the
trim together first to form a ring and distribute it
evenly around the edge. When you sew it onto the
cushion the extra fur will disappear. Fold around the
wound edges and secure with pins. Sew with small
tacking (basting) stitches through all four layers.

Traditional eight-petal rose

Materials
Natural coloured wool: 67 x 62cm (56½ x 54½in)

Yarn
Sterk from Du Store Alpakka
(alpaca/merino wool/nylon)
150g (5½oz) sheep white no. 806

3.5mm (size 4) needles

Finished size: 50 x 60cm (20 x 24in)

To create the front panel, CO 136sts, work 2 rows knit, then work 34sts from graph, but knit the first and last 2sts to form garter stitch border. Repeat to create the back panel, but purl the first and last 2sts.

NB: Read the diagram from right to left on the first row and knit black squares p and white squares k.

Knit the next row in the opposite way: read the diagram from left to right and knit black squares k and white squares p.

Alternative description for the first two rows:
Row 1: K2 *k1, p3, k3, p3, k3, p3, k1, p3, k3, p3, k3, p3*. Repeat from *to * to the end of the row. Finish with k2.
Row 2: P2 *p1, k3, p3, k1, p3, k3, p1, k1, p1, k3, p3, p1, k3, p3, p1, k1*. Repeat from * to * to the end of the row. Finish with p2.

Assembly:
Sew in all loose threads. Press (iron) the work carefully. Place knitted front and back right sides together and sew the pillow with fold (see Good Advice).

Among the oldest knitted garments we know of in Norway are the so-called nightshirts from the 1600s. They were knitted in a very thin silk yarn and the pattern usually featured eight-petalled roses in purl on a knitted bottom. The garments were highly exquisite with finely detailed wire embroidery around the necks. I have tried to revive this 400 year old tradition back with this rose decorated pillow.

The love letter

Finished size: 40 x 50cm (16 x 20in)

Find the middle of the front of the linen and the middle of the pattern and follow the pattern (see Patterns). Sew using 3 threads of Mouliné fine yarn over 2 x 2 threads.

Materials

Front:
Natural coloured linen 42 x 52cm (16½ x 20¾in)

Back:
Natural coloured linen, 33 x 52cm (13 x 20¾in) and 13 x 52cm (5 x 20¾in)
Zip 40cm (16in)

Yarn

DMC mouliné fine yarn
2 skeins of dark brown no. 838

Assembly

Press (iron) the work carefully from the inside. Sew the zip on the back (see Good Advice). Place front and back right sides together. Sew around all four sides. Open the zip. Press (iron) the seams away from each other and cut off the excess fabric in the corners. Reverse the work and press (iron) carefully on the right side.

Romantic rose cushion

Yarn
Mandarin petit from SandnesGarn (cotton)
50g (1¾oz) white no. 1001

White linen: 72 x 22cm (28¾ x 8½in) and
72 x 42cm (28¾ x 16½in) to the front piece,
72 x 42cm (28¾ x 16½in) to the back piece.

3mm (size 11) crochet hook

NB: The pattern measures 12 squares in
width and 21 squares in height.

Finished size: 40 x 70cm (16 x 28in)

In filet crochet you crochet from a diagram.
Each open square equals 1 dc and ch 1.
Every filled square equals ch 2.

Central work:
Row 1: Ch 24.
Row 2: Ch 2 (equals the first dc in the
pattern) + ch 1, then 1 dc in first row's 22.
Ch + ch 1. Continue with 1 dc + ch 1 in every
other row on row 1, the rest of the row. You
should have 12 squares altogether.
Row 3: Ch 2 + 1 and continue as the diagram
shows until you have three roses and four leaves.
When the diagram shows a black square,
crochet 1 dc instead of ch 1.

Finish with one row of open squares
as in the beginning.

Sew in all loose ends, then pin crochet fabric out
to measure 10 x 70cm (4 x 28in). Cover with damp
tea towel and gently press with steam iron or spray
with water – DO NOT SOAK and leave to dry.

Assembly:
Fold the fabrics for the front double (NB: thread
directions the same way) so they measure
11 x 72cm (4¼ x 28½in) and 21 x 72cm (8¼ x 28½in).
Sew along the sides, press (iron) the seams
apart, cut off excess fabric in the corners and
reverse. Press (iron) the work. Attach the finished
central work to the fold of the linen fabric with
pins and sew with a small overstitch. Fold one
of the short edges to the back piece and sew.

Place front and back pieces right sides together
and sew together, leaving one side open.
Press (iron) the seams apart, cut off excess
fabric in the corners and reverse the work.
Crochet 6 cords to tie up with: ch 41,
turn, skip ch 1 and crochet sc back.

Castle with steeples

Materials
White wool fabric: 62 x 52cm (24½ x 20½in)

Yarn
Mitu from Rauma Ullvarefabrikk (alpaca/wool)
100g (3½oz) sheep white no. 0010

3.5mm (size 4) needles

Finished size: 30 x 50cm (12 x 20in)

Diamond Pattern:
To get the diagonals of k st to tilt to the
right or left, the stitches have to switch
places. This is done using a cn.

SR means switch right; place 1 st on cn behind
the work and knit the next 2 sts on the left needle
k before you knit the st on the cn p. This is 3 sts.

SL means switch left; place 2 sts onto the cn in
front of the work and knit 1 st on the left needle
p. Knit the 2 sts on the cn k. This is 3 sts.

CO 110 sts. Knit back and forth.
Row 1 (right side): P4, SR, SL, *p6, SR,
SL*. Repeat from * to * 8 times. The last
4 sts on the needle are knitted p.
Row 2: K4, p2, k2, p2, *k6, p2, k2, p2*.
Repeat from * to * until you have 4 sts left.
The remaining 4 sts are knitted k.
Row 3: P3, SR, p2, SL, *p4, BR, p2,
SL*. Repeat from * to * until you have
3 sts left. They are knitted p.
Row 4: K3, p2, *k4, p2*. Repeat from * to *
until you have 3 sts left. They are knitted k.
Row 5: *P2, SR, p,4 SL*. Repeat from
* to * until you have 2 sts left. They are knitted p.
Row 6: K2, p2, k6, *p2, k2, p2, k6 *. Repeat

from * to * until you have 4 sts left.
They are knitted p2 and k2.
Row 7: P1, *SR, p6, SL*. Repeat from *
to * until you have 1 st left, knitted p.
Row 8: K1, p2, k8, *p4, k8*. Repeat from * to *
until you have 3 sts. They are knitted p2, k1.
Row 9: P1, k2, p8, *place 2 sts on cn behind the
work, knit 2 sts k and then the 2 sts from the cn k,
p8*. Repeat from * to * until you have 3 sts left.
They are knitted k2, p1.
Row 10: As row 8.
Row 11: P1, *SL, p6, SR*. Repeat from
* to * until you have 1 st left, knitted p.
Row 12: As row 6.
Row 13: *P2, SL, p4, SR*. Repeat from * to *
until you have 2 sts left. They are knitted p.
Row 14: As row 4.
Row 15: P3, SL, p2, SR, *p4, SL, p2,
SR*. Repeat from * to * until you have
3 sts left. They are knitted p.
Row 16: As row 2.
Row 17: P4, SL, SR, *p6, SL, SR*.
Repeat from * to * until you have 4
sts left. They are knitted p.
Row 18: K5, p4, *k8, p4*. Repeat from * to *
until you have 5 sts left. They are knitted k.
Row 19: P5, place 2 sts on a cn behind the work,
knit 2 sts k and then the 2 sts from the cn k,
*p8, place 2 sts on a cn behind the work, knit 2
sts k and then the 2 sts k*. Repeat from * to *
until you have 5 sts left. They are knitted p.
Row 20: Repeat row 18.

Repeat these 20 rows 3 times
and then the next 9 rows.

The 9 steeples are made individually:

Row 10 (W.S): K1, p2, k8, p2, k1.
(14 sts on the needle).
Row 11 (R.S): P1, SL, p6, SR, p1
(14 sts on the needle.)
Row 12: K2tog, p2, k6, p2, k2. (You
should have 13 sts on the needle.)

Row 13: P2tog as follows - sl1 purlwise, P1, psso, SL, p4, BS, p1. (You should have 12 sts on the needle.)
Row 14: K2toq, p2, k4, p2, k2. (You should have 11 sts on the needle.)
Row 15: P2tog, SL, p2, SR, p1. (You should have 10 sts on the needle.)
Row 16: K2tog, p2, k2, p2, k2. (You should have 9 sts on the needle.)
Row 17: SL, SR, p1. (You should have 8 sts on the needle.)
Row 18: K2tog, p4, k2. (You should have 7 sts on the needle.)
Row 19: P2tog. Place 1 st on a cn in front of the work, knit 1 st on the left needle p. Then knit the st from the cn k. Place 1 st on a cn behind the work, knit 1 st on the left needle k before you knit st from cn p. (You should have 6 sts on the needle.)
Row 20: Ktog2, p2, k2. (You should have 6 sts on the needle.)

Row 21: P2tog, k2, p2. (You should have 5 sts on the needle.)
Row 22: Ktog2, p2, k1. (You should have 4 sts on the needle.)
Row 23: Cast (bind) off.

Assembly:
Sew in all loose ends. Fold in 14cm (5½in) of the wool fabric at the bottom and 10cm (4in) at the top, place the knitted front and back pieces right sides together and secure with pins. Sew around at the edge of the work, leaving an opening at the bottom. Sew by hand or with a machine.

Cut off excess fabric between the steeples and reverse the work. Fill the steeples with carded wool so they stand up.

This beautiful leaf pattern is called "tuntreet" and it is a 200 year old classic.

Traditional tuntreet

Materials
Felted wool fabric, 60 x 60cm (24 x 24in)
Zip 50cm (20in)

Yarn
Alpaca from Schackenmayr (alpaca)
250g (9oz) sheep white no. 00002

3.5mm (size 4) needles

Finished size: 60 x 60cm (24 x 24in)

Tuntreet:
W is when one st is made into two. This can be done in several different ways. Here I have knitted an extra st in the st of the last row.
A Reduce the amount of sts by taking one st off carefully, knitting one st and lifting the previous st back over.
B Reduce the amount of sts by knitting 2 sts together.
S Reduce the amount of sts by taking one st off carefully, knitting two sts and lifting the previous st back over.

CO 3 sts.
Row 1 (right side): P1, k1, k1
Row 2: W, p1, W.
Row 3: P2, k1, p2.
Row 4: W, k1, p1, k1, W.
Row 5: P3, k1, p3.
Row 6: W, k2, p1, k2, W.
Row 7: P4, yo1, k1, yo1, p4.
Row 8: W, k3, p3, k3, W.
Row 9: K1, p4, k1, yo1, k1, yo1,k1, p4, k1.
Row 10: W, k4, p5, k4, W.

Row 11: P1, k1, p4, k2, yo1, k1, yo1, k2, p4, k1, p1.
Row 12: W, p1, k4, p7, k4, p1, W.
Row 13: P2, k1, p4, k3, yo1, k1, yo1, k3, p4, k1, p2.
Row 14: W, k1, p1, k4, p9, k4, p1, k1, W.
Row 15: P3, k1, p4, k4, yo1, k1, yo1, k4, p4, k1, p3.
Row 16: W, k2, p1, k4, p11, k4, p1, k2, W.
Row 17: P4, yo1, k1, yo1, p4, A, k7, B, p4, yo1, k1, yo1, p4.
Row 18: W, k3, p3, k4, p9, k4, p3, k3, W.
Row 19: K1, p4, k1, yo1, k1, yo1, k1, p4, A, k5, B, p4, k1, yo1, k1, yo1, k1, p4, k1.
Row 20: W, k4, p5, k4, p7, k4, p5, k4, W.
Row 21: P1, k1, p4, k2, yo1, k1, yo1, k2, p4, A, k3, B, p4, k2, yo1, k1, yo1, k2, p4, k1, p1.
Row 22: W, p1, k4, p7, k4, p5, k4, p7, k4, p1, W.
Row 23: P2, k1, p4, k3, yo1, k1, yo1, k3, p4, A, k1, B, p4, k3, yo1,k1, yo1, k3, p4, k1, p2.
Row 24: W, k1, p1, k4, p9, k4, p3, k4, p9, k4, p1, k1, W.
Row 25: P3, k1, p4, k4, yo1, k1, yo1, k4, p4, S, p4, k4, yo1, k1, yo1, k4, p4, k1, p3.
Row 26: W, k2, p1, k4, p11, k4, p1, k4, p11, k4, p1, k2, W.
Row 27: P4, yo1, k1, yo1, p4, A, k7, B, p4, k1, p4, A, k7, B, p4, yo1, k1, yo1, p4.
Row 28: W, k3, p3, k4, p9, k4, p1, k4, p9, k4, p3, k3, W.
Row 29: K1, p4, k1, yo1, k1, yo1, k1, p4, A, k5, B, p4, k1, p4, A, k5, B, p4, k1, yo1, k1, yo1, k1, p4, k1.

Row 30: W, k4, p5, k4, p7, k4, p1, k4, p7, k4, p5, k4, W.

Row 31: P1, k1, p4, k2, yo1, k1, yo1, k2, p4, A, k3, B, p4, k1, p4, A, k3, B, p4, k2, yo1, k1, yo1, k2, p4, k1, p1.

Row 32: W, p1, k4, p7, k4, p5, k4, p1, k4, p5, k4, p7, k4, p1, W.

Row 33: P2, k1, p4, k3, yo1, k1, yo1, k3, p4, A, k1, B, p4, k1, p4, A, k1, B, p4, k3, yo1, k1, yo1, k3, p4, k1, p2.

Row 34: W, k1, p1, k4, p9, k4, p3, k4, p1, k4, p3, k4, p9, k4, p1, k1, W.

Row 35: P3, k1, p4, k4, yo1, k1, yo1, k4, p4, S, p4, k1, p4, S, p4, k4, yo1, k1, yo1, k4, p4, k1, p3.

Row 36: W, k2, p1, k4, p11, k9, p1, k9, p11, k4, p1, k2, W.

Row 37: P4, yo1, k1, yo1, p4, A, k7, B, p9, yo1, k1, yo1, p9, A, k7, B, p4, yo1, k1, yo1, p4.

Row 38: W, k3, p3, k4, p9, k9, p3, k9, p9, k4, p3, k3, W.

Row 39: P5, k1, yo1, k1, yo1, k1, p4, A, k5, B, p9, k1, yo1, k1, p1, k1, p9, A, k5, B, p4, k1, yo1, k1, yo1, k1, p5.

Row 40: W, k4, p5, k4, p7, k9, p5, k9, p7, k4, p5, k4, W.

Row 41: P6, k2, yo1, k1, yo1, k2, p4, A, k3, B, p9, k2, yo1, k1, yo1, k2, p9, A, k3, B, p4, k2, yo1, k1, yo1, k2, p6.

Row 42: W, k5, p7, k4, p5, k9, p7, k9, p5, k4, p7, k5, W.

Row 43: P7, k3, yo1, k1, yo1, k3, p4, A, k1, B, p9, k3, yo1, k1, yo1, k3, p9, A, k1, B, p4, k3, yo1, k1, yo1, k3, p7.

Row 44: W, k6, p9, k4, p3, k9, p9, k9, p3, k4, p9, k6, W.

Row 45: P8, k4, yo1, k1, yo1, k4, p4, S, p9, k4, yo1, k1, yo1, k4, p9, S, p4, k4, yo1, k1, yo1, k4, p8.

Row 46: W, k7, p11, k14, p11, k14, p11, k7, W.

Row 47: P9, A, k7, B, p14, A, k7, B, p14, A, k7, B, p9.

Row 48: P9, A, k7, B, p14, A, k7, B, p14, A, k7, B, p9.

Row 49: P10, A, k5, B, p14, A, k5, B, p14, A, k5, B, p10.

Row 50: W, k9, p7, k14, p7, k14, p7, k9, W.

Row 51: P11, A, k3, B, p14, A, k3, B, p14, A, k3, B, p11.

Row 52: W, k10, p5, k14, p5, k14, p5, k10, W.

Row 53: P12, A, k1, B, p14, A, k1, B, p14, A, k1, B, p12.

Row 54: W, k11, p3, k14, p3, k14, p3, k11, W.

Row 55: P13, S, p14, S, p14, S, p13.

Row 56: W knit k to the end of the needle, finish with W.

Continue with p sts on the right side and k sts on the wrong side as well as CO on every knit row as in row 56. Continue until it measures 30cm (12in).

Knit four equal triangles.

Leaves:
Row 1 (right side): P1, k1, p1.
Row 2: K1, p1, k1.
Row 3: P1, yo1, k1, yo1, p1.
Row 4: K1, p3, k1.
Row 5: p1, k1, yo1, k1, yo1, k1, p1.
Row 6: K1, p5, k1.
Row 7: P1, k2, yo1, k1, yo1, k2, p1.
Row 8: K1, p7, k1.
Row 9: P1, k3, yo1, k1, yo1, k3, p1.
Row 10: K1, p9, k1.
Row 11: P1, k4, yo1, k1, yo1, k4, p1.
Row 12: K1, p11, k1.
Row 13: P1, k5, yo1, k1, yo1, k5, p1.
Row 14: K1, p13, k1.
Row 15: P1, K6, yo1, k1, yo1, k6, p1.
Row 16: K1, p15, k1.
Row 17: P1, k15, p1.
Repeat row 16 and 17 until the leaf measures 13cm (5in).
Then decrease the amount of sts by casting off 1 st on each side every other row (when you are on the right side) like this:
P1, A, k13 k, B, p1.
P1, A, k11, B, p1.
P1, A, k9, B, p1.
P1, A, k7, B, p1.
P1, A, k5, B, p1.
P1, A, k3, B, p1.
P1, A, k1, B, p1.
P1, S, p1.

Cast (bind) off.
Knit four equal leaves.

Lace trim:
CO 5 sts.
Row 1: Knit k back.
Row 2: Knit k1, yo1, k2tog, k1, yo1, k1.
Row 3: Knit k back.
Row 4: Knit k2, yo1, k2tog, k1, yo1, k1.
Row 5: Knit k back.
Row 6: Knit k3, yo1, k2tog, k1, yo1, k1.
Row 7: Knit k back.
Row 8: Knit k4, yo1, k2tog, k1, yo1, k1.
Row 9: Knit k back.
Row 10: Knit k5, yo1, k2tog, k1, yo1, k1.
Row 11: Knit k back.
Row 12: Knit k6, yo1, k2tog, k1, yo1, k1.
Row 13: Knit k back.
Row 14: Knit k7, yo1, k2tog, k1, yo1, k1.
Row 15: Knit k back at the same time as you cast (bind) off the first 8 sts on the needle so you are left with 5 sts.

Repeat Rows 2–15 until you have 40 reports.

Assembly:
Sew in loose ends, and carefully press (iron) the back of the work without making it completely flat. Alternatively block the lace (see Good Advice) with pins and water. Let it dry while blocked out.

Sew the four parts forming the tree together, no further than about 18cm (7in) from the centre. Sew a leaf in every corner. Place the lace and front piece right sides together, pin and sew together.

Cut a hole for the zip, about 12cm (4in) from the top edge and sew it on. Felted wool does not unravel so it does not need to be folded. Place the front and back pieces right sides together, pin and sew together.

Cable-patterned bolster

Yarn
Alpaca from Schackenmayr (alpaca)
150g (5½oz) sheep white no. 00002

3.5mm (size 4) needles

Finished size: 60cm (24cm) long

CO 140 sts on a circular needle. Knit 2 rounds
of moss stitch, first k1, p1 until the end of the
row, then p1, k1 until the end of the row.

Rows 1–3: *P4, k16, p4, k4*.
Repeat from * to * until end of row.
Row 4: *p4, k16, p4, 2 sts are placed on a cn in front
of the work, knit the next 2 sts k, then the 2 sts on
the cn k. Repeat from * to * until the end of the row.
Rows 5–7: Repeat row 1.
Row 8: *P4, 4 sts are placed on a cn in front of
the work, knit the next 4 sts k, then the 4 sts on
the cn k, 4 sts are placed on a cn in front of the
work, knit the next 4 sts k, then the 4 sts on the
cn k, p4, 2 sts are placed on a cn in front of the
work, knit the next 2 sts k, then the 2 sts on the
cn k*. Repeat from * to * until the end of the row.

Rows 9–11: Repeat row 1.
Row 12: Repeat row 4.
Rows 13–15: Repeat row 1.
Row 16: *P4, k4, 4 sts are placed on a cn behind
the work, knit the next 4 sts k, then the 4 sts on
the cn k, k4, p4, 2 sts are placed on a cn in front of
the work, knit the next 2 sts k, then the 2 sts on the
cn k*. Repeat from * to * until the end of the row.
Repeat the pattern a total of 13 times. Then, knit
rows 1–4 and row 2 as 1. Knit k2tog, yo1 until the
end of the row, work 5 rows k and cast (bind) off.
The work should measure about 75cm (30in).

String:
CO 4 sts and knit k. When you finish the needle,
tighten the wire on the back of the work and
knit 1 new row k without turning the work.
Continue until it measures about 90cm (35in).

Assembly:
Sew in loose ends. Tack (baste) with double thread
along the bottom edge and pull as much as possible
so it becomes a fixed ring with a diameter of
about 3.5cm (1½in). Attach the thread securely.
Make a fold along the top edge and thread
the string. Make tassels for the ends.

Upcycled jacket pillow

Finished size: 40 x 60cm (16 x 24in)

Use a sharp knife to open out the seams of an old jacket to obtain flat pieces. See if it will be possible to preserve and reuse any interesting details, such as pockets and buttons. Use a tape measure and an angled ruler and consider how to make the most of the different parts. Mark with a pencil before cutting.

For this grey pillow I used the largest sections from the top of the jacket. The back piece is made from the back of the jacket. The buttoning from the front of the jacket is used as the front piece of the pillow. This avoids finding another way of closing the pillow.

Place fur sides together, keeping in place with pins if necessary. Use a sharp sewing needle or alternatively a small leather needle and buttonhole thread. Attach the thread and tack (baste) a little piece inside the edge. If you use a leather needle you will have to be careful not to cut the leather.

Here we used masking tape to help to get the seams straight, about 1cm (⅜in) from the edge.

Union jack

Finished size: 40 x 40cm (16 x 16in)
See diagram in Patterns section.

Overstitch around the evenweave before you start embroidering. Find the centre of the fabric and start with the black crown, about 8cm (3¼in) from the top. Sew using half cross stitches without tightening the thread too much.

It might be advantageous to finish the crown before you fill with the other colours. Continue until the entire piece is filled with stitches. The evenweave may stretch a little while working. Stretch and pull on the fabric as you go. When the embroidery is finished, block it as described in Good Advice.

Assembly:
Sew the zip on the back piece as described in Good Advice. Place the front and back pieces right sides together. Sew around all four edges. Open the zip. Press (iron) the seams apart and cut off the excess fabric in the corners. Reverse the pillow and press (iron) gently on the right side.

Marius in our hearts

Materials
White wool felt: A piece that measures
43 x 43cm (17 x 17in), one that measures
43 x 27cm (17 x 10¾in), and one that
measures 43 x 16cm (17 x 6¼in)
Zip 35cm (14in)

Yarn
Smart from SandnerGarn (wool)
50g (1¾oz) sheep white no. 1002
50g (1¾oz) blue no. 5575
50g (1¾oz) red no. 4108

3.5mm (size 4) needles

Finished size: 40 x 40cm (16 x 16in)

Use an old Marius sweater or CO 82 sts on a
circular needle with blue yarn and knit 4cm (1½in)
k. Knit 76 sts k from the diagram in the Patterns
section and 6 extra sts k either side of the diagram
in blue or white. You will cut this out later.
Finish by knitting 4cm (1½in) k with red yarn.

Sew with a machine on each side of the
additional sts and cut out. Secure the
loose ends and press (iron) carefully.

Assembly:
NB: See the heart diagram in the Patterns section.
The heart should measure 27cm (10¾in) from one
outer edge to the other.
Sew the zip on the back piece as described in
Good Advice.
Cut out the wool felt with serrated scissors so
both front and back pieces measure 42 x 42cm
(16½ x 16½in). In the front piece, cut out a heart in
the same size and shape as shown in the pattern.

Place the Marius patterned knit work under the
heart so that the pattern is symmetrical around
the centre. Pin and chain stitch 5mm (¼in) inside
the edge using blue yarn. Approximately 1cm (⅜in)
from the blue seam, sew French knots in red.
Place the front and back pieces wrong sides
together. Pin together and tack (baste) in blue,
approximately 1cm (⅜in) inside the
edge. Sew a seam with chain stitch in
red on the inside of the blue seam.

MA-RI-US

Finished size: 30 x 50cm (12 x 20in)

Overstitch around the fabric before you begin.
Place the piece of fabric with the right side towards
you. Find the centre of the front width and start
embroidering the red edge 27cm (10¾in) from
the bottom. Follow the diagram opposite.

Assembly:
Sew in the zip as described in Good Advice. Leave
approximately 2cm (¾in) seam allowance. Reverse
the work so the front and back pieces are right
sides together and sew a seam on each side.
Press the seams apart, cut off excess fabric
in the corners and reverse the pillow.

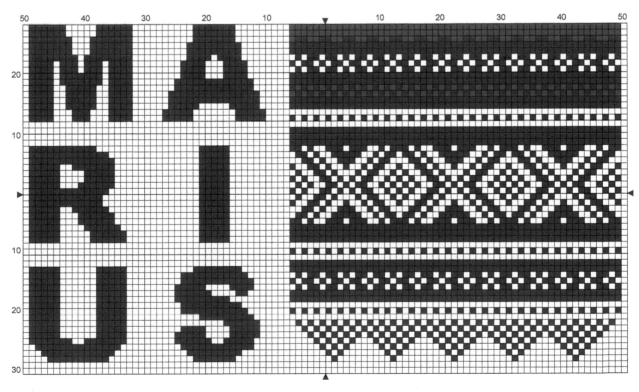

THE DREAM CATCHER

FROM RAGS TO RICHES

Helmer: So you knit?
Mrs. Linde: Of course.
Helmer: Do you know, you ought to embroider?
Mrs. Linde: Really? Why?
Helmer: Yes, it's far more becoming. Let me show you. You hold the embroidery thus in your left hand, and use the needle with the right – like this – with a long, easy sweep. Do you see?
Mrs. Linde: Yes, perhaps –
Helmer: But in the case of knitting – that can never be anything but ungraceful; look here; the arms close together, the knitting needles going up and down – it sort of has a Chinese effect.

This dialogue is taken from Henrik Ibsen's A Doll's House from 1879 and shows very clearly how knitting was not well thought of in finer circles. Although you can find beautiful thin knitted lace from this time period, knitting was first of all seen as a technique for the working class. The technique was used to make garments such as hosiery, socks, sweaters, hats and mittens.

Knitting is known of in Norway from around 1500. Lisbet Pedersdatter is the first knitter we hear about. She was accused of witchcraft and put in jail in Stavanger in 1634. According to the court records, Lisbet had earned a living by knitting stockings for another woman.

In the 1600s there were many working class girls who were trained in practical skills in addition to learning to read in the Catechism. But it was not until the 1700s that the technique really became popular.

From the mid 1800s until the 1970s pretty much every woman in Norway was a knitter. Many have struggled with tight stitches and greasy fingers, but because knitting was a necessity to clothe the family, most women gained great expertise in the subject.

Until the mid 1850s, they pretty much only knitted in one colour. Pattern was primarily created using k and p interchangeably. From Selbu, we know that Marit Gulsetbua, later Emstad, knitted in two colours in the summer of 1857. Then she made a pair of patterned mittens while she was in the mountains with the sheep. She used two different yarns in the work and the subject was a rose. It is said that the mittens were given to Jo Kjøsnes who liked them very much. When Marit and her sisters showed up to church with two-coloured mittens the winter after, they attracted a lot of attention.

The technique of using two different threads was adopted elsewhere in the country about the same time, perhaps even earlier in Rogaland and Hordaland. From the Faroe Islands, the technique is know all the way back to the 1700s. The technique presented the opportunity to make warmer and thicker garments, but also the possibility of decorative patterns. The mittens, socks, hats, and jerseys that were plain before all became decorated in assorted patterns. Different parts of the country had special characteristics. We know the difference between a fana jumper and a setesdal sweater, and most know the term selbu-pattern. Selbu-knit is still used as a term for black and white patterned knitting abroad.

Beware of crumbs in the couch! American cupcakes with sweet icing have lately worked their way into the Norwegian kitchen. It is no longer enough to just make cupcakes. They must also be decorated; each one better than the other. They need to taste sweet and look sweet.

Cupcakes

Materials
Natural coloured linen:
67 x 52cm (26½ x 20¾in) for the front and
52 x 52cm (20¾ x 20¾in) for the back.

Yarn
Mandarin Petit from Sandnes (cotton):
50g (1¾oz) pink no. 4505
50g (1¾oz) white no. 17
50g (1¾oz) red no. 4418
Pandora from Rauma Ullvarefabrikk (cotton):
50g (1¾oz) pink no. 232

3.25mm (size 3) needles
3.25mm (size 3) crochet hooks

Finished size: 50 x 50cm (20 x 20in)

Cupcakes:
Row 1: CO 21 sts with pink yarn.
Row 2: Knit k1, p1 to the end of
the needle. Finish with k1.
Row 3: Knit back p1, k1 to the end of the needle.
Finish with p1.
Row 4: Repeat row 2.
Row 5: Repeat row 3.
Row 6: Knit k1, CO p1, knit p1,
k1, p1. Repeat from * to * 8 times,
k1, CO p1, knit p1, k1. (Now you should
have 23 sts on the needle.)
Row 7: Knit back p1, k2, *p1, k1*.
Repeat from * to * 8 times, p1, k2, p1.
Row 8: Knit k1, p2, *k1, p1*. Repeat
from * to * 8 times, k1, p2, k1.
Row 9: Repeat row 7.

Row 10: Knit k1, p2, k1, CO p1, knit p1,
k1, p1. Repeat from * to * 6
times, k1, CO p1, knit p1, k1,
p2, k1. (25 sts on the needle).
Row 11: Knit back *p1, k2*. Repeat from * to * twice.
k1, p1. Repeat from * to * 6 times,
p1, k2. Repeat from * to * twice, p1.
Row 12: Knit *k1, p2*. Repeat from * to * twice,
p1, k1. Repeat from * to * 6 times,
p1, k2. Repeat from * to * twice, p1.
Row 13: Repeat row 11.
Row 14: Knit *k1, p2*.
Repeat from * to * twice, k1, CO p1, knit p1,
k1, p1. Repeat from * to * 4 times,
k1, CO p1, knit p1,
k1, p2. Repeat from * to * twice,
k1 (27 sts on the needle).
Row 15: Knit back *p1, k2*.
Repeat from * to * 3 times,
p1, k1. Repeat from * to * 4 times,
p1, k2. Repeat from * to * 3 times, p1.
Row 16: Knit *k1, p2*.
Repeat from * to * 3 times, knit k1, CO p1, p1,
k1, p1. Repeat from * to * twice,
k1, CO p1, p1, *k1, p2*.
Repeat from * to * 3 times, k1.
(29 sts on the needle).
Row 17: Knit back *p1, k2*
Repeat from * to * 4 times,
p1, k1. Repeat from * to * twice,
p1, k2. Repeat from * to * 4 times, p1.
Row 18: Knit *k1, p2*. Repeat from * to * 4 times,
knit k1, CO p1, knit p1, k1, CO p1, knit p1,
k1, p2. Repeat from * to * 4 times,
k1 (31 sts on needle).
Row 19: Knit back *p1, k2*. Repeat
from * to * 10 times, p1.

Row 20: Switch to white yarn and knit k.
Row 21: Knit p back.
Row 22: Knit k4, tk2 together, k8, tk2 together, k9, k2tog, k4. (28 sts on needle).
Row 23: Repeat row 21.
Row 24: Knit k4, tk2 together, k4, tk2 together, k4, k2tog, k4, k2tog, k4. (24 sts on the needle).
Row 25: Repeat row 21.
Row 26: Knit k4, tk2 together, k3, tk2 together, k2, k2tog, k3, k2tog, k4. (20 sts on the needle).
Row 27: Repeat row 21.
Row 28: Knit k4, tk2 together, k2, tk2 together, k2tog, k2, k2tog, k4. (16 sts on the needle).
Row 29: Repeat row 21.
Row 30: Knit tk2 together, k2, tk2 together, k4, k2tog, k2, k2tog. (12 sts on the needle).
Row 31: Repeat row 21.
Row 32: Knit tk2 together, k1, tk2 together, k2, k2tog, k1, k2tog. (8 sts on the needle).
Row 33: Repeat row 21.
Row 34: Knit k2, tk2 together, k2tog, k2. (6 sts on the needle).
Row 35: Repeat row 21.
Row 36: Switch to red yarn and knit k.
Row 37: Repeat row 21.
Row 38: Knit tk2 together, k2, k2tog. (4 sts on the needle)
Row 39: Repeat row 21.
Row 40: Cast (bind) off.

Attach the loose ends.

Fold the red cherry on top gently inwards so that it rounds off for a nice finishing touch. You need a row of 5, then 4, then 3 cupcakes – 12 in total. Here, some of the cakes have a dark pink cupcake case, some have light pink and some are striped. It doesn't matter if the cupcakes are not exactly the same. Vary in the way you CO and cast (bind) off.

Lace:
For the cake platter, CO 79, 61, and 49 ch using white yarn.
Row 1: 1ch, sc into 2nd ch from hook, 1sc into each ch to end, turn.
Row 2: 1sl st into 1st st, *skip 2ch, 6dc into next st*, rep from * to * to the end of row. Break off yarn.
For outer edge trim make 457 ch and work as given above. The lace will then be 2m (2 yds) and have 19 x 4 loops.

Assembly:
These cupcakes are sewn onto a solid piece of light grey linen canvas. Use your imagination; you can use almost anything! One alternative is to use a knitted background. Start with the bottom lace and place it about 8.5cm (3½in) from the bottom edge. Use a 15cm (6in) fold. Sew along the top edge with small invisible stitches. Place five cakes evenly out, starting with the middle cake. Cut out a small piece of cotton wool and place it inside the cake before you sew it on to the bottom with small stitches. This will give the cakes a three dimensional shape. When the first row is complete, place the next lace a little above it and sew it on. Continue in this way until all the cakes are in place.

Decorate the cupcakes with small glass beads sewn on with small stitches.

Make the pillow with fold (see Good Advice).

Sew the lace around the pillow. It should have 19 loops on each side.

Spiral pillow

Yarn
Allino from BC Garn (cotton/linen)
250g (9oz) light purple no. 13

3.5mm (size 4) crochet hooks

Finished work: 50cm (20in) in diameter

Crochet 5 ch and make into a circle with 1 sl st.
Row 1: Crochet 2 ch and continue with
dc around the circle, total 12 sts.
Use a stitch marker to mark where the row
starts and ends. Crochet dc in a thread you pick
up on the backside of the work, so that sts from
the previous row are in the front of the
work as a row of sl st. Continue in the
same direction the whole time.
Row 2: Crochet 1 sc first, then 1 dc.
Continue with 2 dc in every st, so
you get a total of 24 sts.
Row 3: *2 dc in first st and 1 dc in next st*.
Repeat from * to * until the end of the row.
Row 4: *1 dc into next 2 sts, then 2 dc in the next st*.
Repeat from * to * until the end of the row.
Row 5: *1 dc into next 3 sts, then
2 dc in next st*. Repeat from * to * until
the end of the row and the next row.
Row 6: *1 dc into next 4 sts, then
2 dc in next st*. Repeat from
* to * until the end of the row.
Row 7: *1 dc into next 5 sts, then
2 dc in next st*. Repeat from
* to * until the end of the row.
Row 8: *1 dc into next 6 sts, then
2 dc in next st*. Repeat from
* to * until the end of the row.
Row 9: *1 dc into next 7 sts, then
2 dc in next st*. Repeat from
* to * until the end of the row.
Row 10: *1 dc into next 8 sts, then
2 dc in next st*. Repeat from
* to * until the end of the row.
Row 11: *1 dc into next 9 sts, then
2 dc in next st*. Repeat from
* to * until the end of the row.
Row 12: *1 dc into next 10 sts, then
2 dc in next st*. Repeat from
* to * until the end of the row.
Crochet next row.
Row 13: *1 dc into next 12 sts, then
2 dc in next st*. Repeat from
* to * until the end of the row.
Row 14: *1 dc into next 14 sts, then
2 dc in next st*. Repeat from
* to * until the end of the row.
Row 15: *1 dc into next 16 sts, then
2 dc in next st*. Repeat from * to
* until the end of the row.
Row 16: *1 dc into next 18 sts, then
2 dc in next st*. Repeat from
* to * until the end of the row.
Row 17: *1 dc into next 20 sts, then
2 dc in next st*. Repeat from
* to * until the end of the row.
Row 18: *1 dc into next 25 sts, then
2 dc in next st*. Repeat from
* to * until the end of the row.
Row 19: *1 dc into next 30 sts, then
2 dc in next st* Repeat from
* to * until the end of the row.
Row 20: *1 dc into next 35 sts, then
2 dc in next st*. Repeat from
* to * until the end of the row.
Row 21: *1 dc into next 40 sts, then
2 dc in next st*. Repeat from
* to * until the end of the row.
Row 22: *1 dc into next 45 sts, then
2 dc in next st*. Repeat from
* to * until the end of the row.
Row 23: *1 dc into next 50 sts, then
2 dc in next st*. Repeat from
* to * until the end of the row.
Row 24: No increase.
Row 25: *1 dc into next 60 sts, then
2 dc in next st*. Repeat from
* to * until the end of the row.
Row 26: *1 dc into next 70 sts, then 2 dc in next
st*. Repeat from * to * until the end of the row.
Row 27: No increase.

The work should now be approximately 50cm (20in) in diameter.
Make the back piece in the same way.

Assembly:
Place the two pieces wrong sides together and crochet together with sc. Leave about 25cm (10cm) for the pillow. Make the lace trim like this: *1 sc, 3 ch and 1 sc into the third st*.

Repeat from * to * until the end of the row. Crochet then 1 sc, 3 dc and 1 ch in every loop until the end of the row. Secure all loose ends.

Make a button closure (see Good Advice) or sew together.

Pretty in pink

Materials
Fabric for back piece:
62 x 47cm (54½ x 18½in)

Yarn
Lerke from Dale Garn (merino wool/cotton)
100g (3½oz) light pink no. 3811
Allino from BC garn (linen)
50g (1¾oz) light purple no. 13
Louisa from Y (silk)
50g (1¾oz) mulberry 06 pink
Spin silk with beads & sequins (silk)
50g (1¾oz) hibiscus

3.5mm (size 4) crochet hooks

Finished size: 45 x 45cm (18 x 18in)

Work 101ch with light pink Lerke and make into a
ring with a sl st. Crochet sc from the diagram in
the Patterns section, 95 sts. See Good Advice for
tips on how to crochet sc with multiple colours.
Read the diagram from right to left, bottom to
top, just like when you are knitting. The extra

6 sts are always crocheted with light pink.
The work might stretch and become crinkled
when you crochet but this will disappear when
you block and work on it once you have finished.

The yarn follows you all the way around; the
yarn you don't use in the sc are hidden inside
the st. Make sure not to tighten these threads.
This will make the work uneven very easily.

You may want to colour the rows you have
finished as you work along. This will make it
easier to know where you are at any time.

Continue until you have finished the diagram.

Assembly:
Attach all loose ends and use a machine to sew
a tight zigzag on each side of the central stitch
in the light pink area. Cut the pieces apart.

Block the work with pins (see Good Advice).

Find a suitable fabric for the back piece.
Here I've used light pink corduroy. Sew
the pillow with fold (see Good Advice).

Lace thick knit

Yarn
Hubro from Dale Garn (wool)
700g (1lb 9oz) pearl pink no. 3810

9mm (size 13) needles

Finished size: 50 x 70cm (20 x 28in)

CO 180 sts on a circular needle.
Round 1: Purl the whole way around.
Round 2: *K1, p3, k1, p3, k1, p3, k1, p3, k2*. Repeat these 18 sts from * to* the whole way around, in total 10 times.
Round 3: *Yo1, k1, p2tog, k1, p3, k1, p3, k1, p1, p2tog, k1, yo1, k1*.
Repeat from * to * the whole way around.
Round 4: *K2, p2, k1, p3, k1, p3, k1, p2, k3*.
Repeat from * to * the whole way around.
Round 5: *K1, yo1, k1, p2, k1, p2tog, p1, k1, p1, p2tog, k1, p2, k1, yo1, k2*.
Repeat from * to * the whole way around.
Round 6: *K3, p2, k1, p2, k1, p2, k1, p2, k4*.
Repeat from * to * the whole way around.
Round 7: *K2, yo1, k1, p2tog, k1, p2, k1, p2, k1, p2tog, k1, yo1, k3*.
Repeat from * to * the whole way around.
Round 8: *K4, p1, k1, p2, k1, p2, k1, p1, k5*.
Repeat from * to * the whole way around.
Round 9: *K3, yo1, k1, p1, k1, p2tog,

k1, p2tog, k1, p1, k1, yo1, k4*.
Repeat from * to * the whole way around.
Round 10: *K5, p1, k1, p1, k1, p1, k1, p1, k6*.
Repeat from * to * the whole way around.
Round 11: *K4, p2tog, p2tog, k1, p2tog, p2tog, k5*. Repeat from * to * the whole way around.
The work should now have 14 sts and you should have 140 sts left on the needle
Round 12: Purl the whole way around.
Round 13: *Yo1, k2tog*.
Repeat from * to * the whole way around.
Round 14: Knit the whole way around.
Round 15: Purl the whole way around.

Continue working in knit until work measures 40cm (16in). Cast (bind) off 70 sts and continue with moss stitch (k1, p1 first round, p1, k1 second round) on the back piece for 4 rounds before you cast (bind) off the last 70 sts.

Knit another lace trim but once you finish round 15, continue with 3 rounds of k before you cast (bind) off.

Assembly:
Sew the loose lace trim onto the rest of the pillow so that the moss stitching is underneath. Leave an opening of about 40cm (16in) in the centre. Crochet 6 strings of 15 ch that you tie the opening with, or attach 4 buttons, 3–3.5cm (1¼–1½in) in diameter, and use the hole ending as buttonholes. Sew the lace trim onto each side.

Pink meadow

Yarn
Hubro from Dale Garn (wool)
700g (1lb 9oz) pearl pink no. 3810

9mm (size 13) needles

The front piece of this pillow is put together with a total of 30 Japanese flowers and 20 small granny squares that fill the holes between the flowers.

Japanese flower:
Roound 1: Crochet 4 ch with pink yarn and make a ring with 1 sl st.
Round 2: Begin with 3 ch, which is the same as 1 dc and 1 ch, and continue with 1 dc and 1 ch until you have 12 dc into the ring. Finish with 1 sl st in 1 ch.
Round 3: Begin with 4 lm, which is the same as 1 dc and 2 ch. Continue with 1 dc around the ch loop from the last round and 2 ch to the end of the round. Finish with 1 sl st in 1 ch.
Round 4: Begin with 2 ch, which is the same as 1 dc, and crochet 3 dc more in the same loop. Continue with 4 dc in every ch loop around until you have 48 dc. Finish with 1 sl st in 1 ch.
Round 5: Begin with 1 sc between first and second dc in the group of 4 dc, *crochet 5 ch, skip 2 dc, 1 sc, skip 2 dc, 1 sc*. Repeat from * to * until the end of the round.
Round 6: *Crochet 8 dc in each ch loop, 1 sc between the 2 sc*. Repeat from * to * until the end of the round.

When you have crocheted almost another flower, crochet the two flowers together. On round 6 crochet *4 dc in the loop, 1 sl st between 4 and 5 dc in the first flower and then 4 dc, 1 sc*. Repeat from * to * so the flowers are attached in two loops.

Crochet six flowers together in a round using this method. When you start the next round you have to attach the flowers in two places. They should have one open loop between them before you apply the next flower.

Squares between the flowers:
Use brown yarn and follow the instructions for Japanese flowers for rounds 1–3.
Round 4: *Crochet 3 sc around the first ch loop, 1 sl st between 4 and 5 dc in one of the available leaves on a pink flower, then 1 sc more in the same loop, 3 sc around the next ch loop, 3 ch, 1 sl st around sl st that holds two pink flowers together, 3 ch*. Repeat from * to * until you have attached the square to four flowers. Pull together with 1 sl st.

Assembly:
Sew in all loose ends. The work should now measure approximately 53 x 64cm (21 x 25in). Pin the work to a neutral background and sew small stitches along the outermost flowers. Sew the zip on the back piece as described in Good Advice.

Cut off excess fabric in the corners. Press (iron) the seams apart and reverse.

Alternatively it is also possible to crochet a back piece that is exactly the same and then crochet the two pieces together using sc around the edge.

Rose bouquet

Materials
Two round pieces of fabric with a
47cm (18½in) diameter

Yarn
Chiri Alpaca from Rauma Ullvarefabrikk
(alpaca/silk)
150g (5½oz) light pink no. CH 401

4.5mm (size 7) crochet hooks

Finished work: 45cm (18in) in diameter

The flowers are made in two separate steps. First
you will make the base and then the spiral that
forms the petals. In total you will need 22 roses.

Base:
Crochet 5 ch and make a ring with one sl st.
Round 1: Crochet 2 ch and continue with
dc around the ring, total 12 dc.
Use a stitch holder to help you see where the
rounds start and end. Continue crocheting dc
with a thread you pick up from the backside
of the work, so that the st from the last round
are in the front of the work as a round of sl st.
Continue in the same direction the whole time.
Round 2: Crochet 1 sc, then 1 dc.
Continue with 2 dc in each st, total 24 sts.
Round 3: In the next round, crochet *2
dc in first st and 1 dc in the next st*.
Repeat from * to * until the end of the round.
Round 4: Continue with *1 dc in each st
2 times, then 2 dc in the next st*.
Repeat from * to * until the end of the round.
End with 1 sc and then 1 sl st.

Rose spiral:
Crochet 14 ch, turn, crochet first dc into the third
st. Continue with dc back. You should have 13 dc.
Then yo and crochet 1 dc in the first st in the centre
of the base. Continue with 2 dc in each st for 4
rounds. Then you should have one ring with dc left
at the outermost round. Finish with 1 sc and 1 sl st.

Assembly:
Sew the loose string of dc in the middle
of the flower as a natural extension of the
rose spiral. Secure all loose threads.
Place one rose in the middle and sew seven roses
to it in a circle. Make another ring outside of the 14
remaining roses. Secure all loose threads well.
When you have sewn all of the 22 roses together,
the distance between the inner rose and outermost
roses is relatively large. The work will distort a little.
Therefore, attach the outer spiral of the innermost
rose to the spiral of the roses on the outside.

Overstitch around the two pieces of fabric.

Place the roses on top of one of the fabric
pieces and sew along the edge of each rose
using backstitch. Secure all loose ends well.

Then place the front and back pieces right
sides together. Pin all the way around and
sew using a machine until there is about
25cm (10cm) left. Attach the thread well. Set the
machine to a longer stitch length and continue
sewing until you meet the other seam.

Press (iron) the seams apart. Undo the stitches
with the longer stitch length, reverse the
work, pin on the zip and sew. Alternatively,
stitch up the opening with backstitch.

If you want to hide the background fabric so that
only the roses are visible, sew a small tuck of about
1cm (⅜in) between each flower in the seam.

Going bananas

Materials
Front: Natural coloured linen, 7.5 threads per cm, 52 x 52cm (20¾ x 20¾in)
Back: Natural coloured linen, 43 x 52cm (17 x 20¾in) and 13 x 52cm (5 x 20¾in)
Zip 40cm (16in)

Yarn
DMC mouliné fine yarn
Black no. 310, 2 skeins
Light pink no. 603, 2 skeins
Dark pink no. 602, 1 skein
Light yellow no. 743, 2 skeins
Dark yellow no. 972, 1 skein
Light blue no. 598, 2 skeins
Blue no. 807, 1 skein

NB: The pattern is sewn with the whole yarn, which is 6 threads, over 3 x 3 threads.

Finished size: 50 x 50cm (20 x 20in)

Find the centre of the fabric but place the subject as if the centre was 5cm (2in) higher. Follow the diagram below.

Assembly:
Press (iron) the work carefully from the inside. Sew the zip on the back piece (see Good Advice). Place the front and back pieces right sides together. Sew around all four sides. Open the zip. Press (iron) the seams apart and cut off excess fabric in the corners. Reverse the work and press (iron) carefully.

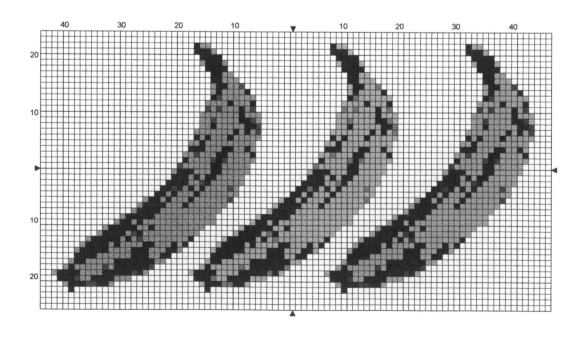

Retro design

Materials
Natural coloured linen. Front piece is cut
approximately 47cm (18½in) in diameter.
Back piece is sewn from two rectangles that
measure 26 x 49cm (10½ x 19½in)
Zip 35cm (14in)

Yarn
PT Petunia from Rauma Ullvarefabrikk
(cotton)
100g (3½oz) white no. 221
50g (1¾oz) pink no. 722

3.5mm (size 4) crochet hooks

Finished size: 45cm (18in) in diameter

Round 1: Crochet 5 ch with pink yarn
and make a ring with 1 sl st.
Round 2: Crochet 2 ch (which is first dc),
1 ch, *1 dc, 1 ch*. Repeat from * to * until you
have a total of 9 dc. Pull together with 1 sl st.
Round 3: Crochet 1 ch in each dc
2 sc around every ch loop.
Round 4: Crochet 2 ch (which is first dc),
1 ch, *3 dc, 1 ch*.
Repeat from * to * 8 times, and finish with 2 dc.
Pull together with 1 sl st.
Round 5: Switch to white yarn. Secure the
thread around a ch loop and crochet 2 ch (which
is first dc), 2 dc around the same ch loop, 3
ch, *3 dc around the next ch loop, 3 ch*.
Repeat from * to * 8 times and
pull together with 1 sl st.
Round 6: Switch back to pink yarn. Secure the
thread around a ch loop and crochet 2 ch (which
is first dc), 2 dc around the same ch loop, 1 dc
between the next two dc, 1 dc between the 2 next dc,
*3 dc in the next ch loop, 1 dc between
the next two dc, 1 dc the 2 next dc*.
Repeat from * to * until the end of the
round and pull together with 1 sl st.
Round 7: Switch to white yarn and crochet 1 sc,
1 ch the whole round. Pull together with 1 sl st.

Round 8: Switch to pink yarn and
crochet 2 sc in every ch loop.
Round 9: Switch to white yarn and crochet sc the
whole round. You should now have 90 sts in total.
Round 10: Crochet sc the whole round.
Round 11: Crochet 1 sc, 3 ch, skip 2
st the whole round. Pull together with 1 sl st.
Round 12: Switch to pink yarn. Secure the thread
around a ch loop and crochet 2 ch (which is
first dc), 2 dc more around the same ch loop.
Continue with 3 dc in each loop until the end
of the round. Pull together with 1 sl st.
Round 13: Switch to white yarn, crochet 1 sc and
4 ch, skip 3 sts the whole round. Sc should be right
above sc in 11 round. Pull together with 1 sl st.
Round 14: Crochet 4 sc in each ch loop.
Round 15: Crochet sc the whole round.
Round 16: Crochet 2 ch (which is first dc),
and continue with 1 dc in each sc to the end
of the round. Pull together with 1 sl st.
Round 17: Switch to pink yarn and
crochet sc the whole round.
Round 18: Switch to white yarn
and ch the whole round.
Round 19: Crochet 2 ch (which is first
dc), and continue with dc to the end of
the round. Pull together with 1 sl st.
Round 20: Secure the thread right above
ch in round 11 and 13, and crochet 2 ch
(which is first dc). Crochet 2 dc more in the
same space, 2 ch, skip 3 sts, *3 dc, 3 ch,
skip 3 st*. Repeat from * to * until the end of
the round and pull together with 1 sl st.
Round 21: Crochet 2 ch (which is first dc)
and then 2 dc more in the same ch loop,
1 dc between the next 2 dc, 1 st between the
next 2 dc, *3 dc around the next ch loop,
1 dc between then next 2 dc, 1 dc between the
next 2 dc*. Repeat from * to * until the end
of the round and pull together with 1 sl st.
Round 22: *1 sc between first and second dc in
the ch loop, 1 ch, 1 sc between second and third
dc in the ch loop, 5 ch*. Repeat from * to * until
the end of the round, pull together with 1 sl st.
Round 23: 1 sc in the small ch loop and 5 sc
in the large ch loop to the end of the round.

Round 24: Crochet 2 ch (which is first in dc), and then 1 dc in each st to the end of the round. Pull together with 1 sl st.

Round 25: 5 sc, then 1 sc down in round 23 over the small ch loop to the end of the round.

Round 26: Skip 1 st, *crochet 1 sc, 5 ch, skip 3 sts, 1 sc, skip 3sts*. Repeat from * to * to the end of the round.

Round 27: Crochet 2 ch (which is first dc) in the large ch loop, and then 3 dc more in the same loop, 3 dc in next ch loop, *4 dc in the large ch loop, 3 dc in the small ch loop*. Repeat from * to * until the end of the round. Pull together with 1 sl st.

Round 28: Crochet 2 ch (which is first dc), *2 dc between second and third dc in the large ch loop then 1 dc between every dc 5 times*. Repeat from * to * until the end of the round, but only 1 dc between each dc 4 times at the end. Pull together with 1 sl st.

Round 29: Switch to pink yarn and crochet 1 sc over 1 of sc in round 26, *5 ch, skip 4 dc, 1 sc*. Repeat from * to * until the end of the round. Pull together with 1 sl st.

Round 30: Crochet * 2 sc around first ch loop, 1 ch, 5 dc around next ch loop, 1 ch *. Repeat from * to * until the end of the round. Pull together with 1 sl st.

Round 31: Switch to white yarn. *Crochet 4 sc around the small ch loop in round 29 so that the pink sc in round 30 are partially covered with white yarn, and then 1 sc around the ch, 1 sc between every dc 4 times, 1 sc around the ch*. Repeat from * to * until the end of the round.

Round 32: Crochet 2 ch (which is first dc), and then 1 dc in each sc until the end of the round. Pull together with 1 sl st.

Round 33: Crochet 3 sc over the pink ch loop that was crocheted from the white yarn, and then 7 dc until the end of the round. Pull together with 1 sl st.

Assembly:
Sew in all loose ends.
Sew the crochet work onto the front piece with a small overstitch on the inside of the last pink edge so that the final 4 rounds are outside the seam.
Sew the zip onto the back piece (see Good Advice).
Cut the back piece so it has the same size as the front piece.

Place the front and back piece right sides together and sew around. Press (iron) the seams apart and reverse the pillow.

SEA SPRAY

DOWN AND FEATHERS

One of man's natural desires is to seek comfort and that is why pillows are one of the oldest decorating tools we know of. Although there is little evidence of old textiles, several old fragments that have been found to be pillows have been discovered in the Oseberg ship, a well-preserved Viking ship happened upon in a large burial mound at the Oseberg farm near Tønsberg, Norway. Haakon Shetelig wrote, "in the tomb there must have been a fine bed with ample supply of duvets, pillows and blankets", when he opened the tomb in 1904. There were remains of wool, linen and silk and examples of complex woven fabrics and impressive embroidery art. The textiles had been underground for more than 1000 years, yet many of them were surprisingly well-preserved and remarkably fresh.

Large amounts of down and feathers that were found in the ship have been said to be, among other things, filling in pillows and duvets. But down was rare and probably a sign of high social status. As early as the 800s, down and feathers were used as means of payment, and material from the 1700s shows that one and a half kilos of down could be worth about as much as a cow.

Pillows were primarily used in the beds, which were made in several ways. Both economic and geographical factors played a role. For mattresses, they used straw or feathers, but also animal fur. The pillows were filled with the finest and softest material they had. To use as a cover, besides duvets, they had pelts and weaved rugs. Many wonder why the beds in the past were so short, but it was common to sleep in a half upright position under the pelt, well-supported by pillows. Many people also slept on the same bed, which made it easier to keep warm in the winter.

For special occasions, when the finest fabrics were hung on the walls, they probably also used pillows on the benches.

The most luxurious material you can use to fill a duvet or a pillow with is light eiderdown. Its insulation is remarkable, which is reflected in its price. One duvet can cost from about four thousand pounds. From one nest you can only obtain about 16g (½oz) of fully cleaned down. To fill an entire duvet you would need down from about 64 nests. For a pillow you would need maybe a quarter of that.

Eiderdown is currently a rare commodity. The collection and cleansing of it is very time-consuming. It takes two to three weeks to clean 1kg (2lb 4oz) of eiderdown by hand. Cleaning the down by hand preserves its main qualities and fine resilience.

The tradition of building nests and houses for the eider duck and gathering the valuable down is still being kept up in Vega in Norway, even though mink have reduced the stock substantially. The bird houses are being built for the ducks to have a place where they can be dry and warm, and if they settle there, they often return year after year. The female plucks down from her breast and to line the nest. The exclusive fibres are gathered when the ducklings are hatched.

Blue anchor

Materials
Zip 30cm (12in)

Yarn
PT Petunia from Rauma Ullvarefabrikk
(cotton)
300g (10½oz) white no. 296
50g (1¾oz) dark blue no. 277

3.5mm (size 4) needles

Finished size: 45 x 45cm (18 x 18in)

Front:
CO 109 sts with white yarn.
Row 1: Purl back.
Row 2: K2, *sl1, p3*. Repeat from * to * until
the end of the needle. Finish with sl1 and k2.
Row 3: Purl back.
Row 4: K2, *sl1, k3*. Repeat from * to * until
the end of the needle. Finish with sl1 and k2.
Row 5: Purl back.
Row 6: Repeat Row 4.
Row 7: P3, *k3, p1*. Repeat from * to * until
the end of the needle. Finish with p2.
Row 8: Repeat Row 4.
Row 9: Purl back.
Row 10: Repeat Row 4.
Row 11: Purl back.

Repeat Rows 2–11 until you have 29 square
rows. The work should then be approximately
44.5cm (18in). Finish with one row as
Row 4. Purl back and cast (bind) off.

Back, lower part:
Follow the same procedure as the front piece,
but once you've knitted 22 square rows, knit
a) Repeat Row 2: k2, *take 1 st off by
sticking the needle from the back into the
st, p3*. Repeat from * to * until the end
of the needle. Finish with sl1 and k2.
b) Knit back as Row 7: P3, *k3, p1 *. Repeat from
* to * until the end of the needle. Finish with p2.
Repeat rows a) and b) and cast (bind) off.

Back, top part:
CO 109 sts in white yarn.
Row 1: Purl back.
Row 2: K2, *take 1 st off by sticking the needle
from the back into the st, p3*. Repeat from * to *
until the end of the needle. Finish with sl1 and k2.
Row 3: P3, *k3, p1*. Repeat from * to * until
the end of the needle. Finish with p2.
Row 4: Repeat row 2.
Row 5: Repeat row 3.
Row 6: K2, *sl1, k3*. Repeat from * to * until
the end of the needle. Finish with sl1 and k2.
Row 7: P3, *k3, p1*. Repeat from * to * until
the end of the needle. Finish with p2.
Row 8: Repeat row 6.
Row 9: Purl back.
Row 10: Repeat row 6.
Row 11: Purl back.
Continue with rows 1–11 as on the front piece,
until you have 7 square rows in total. Finish with
Row 1 as Row 4, purl back and cast (bind) off.

Blue edge:
CO 461 sts with blue yarn on a circular needle
and knit the first round in blue yarn. Continue
the next rounds of 3 blue, 1 white. The st number

should make the pattern shift 1 st to the left creating diagonal stripes. Continue until you have 7 rows of pattern. Cast (bind) off with blue yarn.

Assembly:
Cross stitch with double blue thread on the front piece following the diagram. You should have four white squares under the anchor and three above. The whole square should be covered in stocking stitch.

Secure all loose ends.

Sew the zip on the back plate (see Good Advice).

Place front and back pieces right sides facing and sew or crochet together. Divide the blue edge into four equal parts, pin to front piece and sew. Fold the edge around the seam while you roll it into a tight snake. Pin and sew it to the back piece.

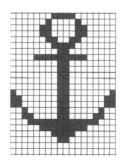

American flag

Materials
14 blue buttons

Yarn
PT Petunia from Rauma Ullvarefabrikk
(cotton)
200g (7oz) white no. 296
100g (3½oz) red no. 256
50g (1¾oz) blue no. 277

3.5mm and 3mm (size 4 and 3) crochet hooks

Finished size 40 x 60cm (16 x 24in)

Using 3.5mm (size 4) crochet hooks: Work 122 ch with red yarn, plus one extra when you turn, and crochet 6 rows sc back and forth. Switch to white yarn and continue with dc. When you turn you have to crochet 2 extra ch, which will be the first dc on the next row. Continue until the work measures 28cm (11in).

Switch back to red yarn and crochet 4 rows dc back and forth. Switch to white yarn and crochet 4 rows back and forth. Continue in this way until you have 3 red and 3 white stripes in the flag.

*Switch back to red, but this time only crochet 74 dc before you switch to blue yarn and crochet the remaining 48 dc. Turn, crochet 48 blue dc and 74 white. Repeat until you have 4 rows of dc in total. Switch to white yarn and crochet 74 white dc and 48 blue, turn and crochet 48 blue and 74 white, repeat these 2 rows until you have

4 rows*. Repeat from * to * 3½ times. The last stripe in the flag should therefore be red. You are now finished with the front piece. Continue with the top part of the back piece by switching to white yarn and crocheting with this for the entire row, 122 sts. Crochet dc back and forth until the back piece measures 12cm (4½in). Switch to red yarn and crochet 3 rows sc. Then crochet 7 sc, *3 ch, skip 3 sc and crochet 6 sc*, repeat from * to * 12 times and finish the row with 7 sc. Next row crochet 7 sc, *3 sc around the ch loop, 6 sc*, repeat from * to * 12 times and finish with 7 sc. Then crochet 2 rows of sc.

Crochet star:
Use white yarn and 3mm (size 3) crochet hook
Round 1: Crochet 4 ch, make a ring with 1 sl st in first ch, 1 ch.
Round 2: Crochet 6 sc in the ring, finish with 1 sl st in first sc, 1 ch.
Round 3: 2 sc in each sc = 12 sc, finish with 1 sl st in first sc, 1 ch.
Round 4: *1 sc, 1 ch (= small star loop), 1 sc in next st, 4 ch, 1 sc in the fourth ch from the needle, 1 ch*, repeat from * to * (= 6 small star loops) finish with 1 sl st in first sc. Cut off the thread and pull through. Crochet 13 stars in total.

Assembly:
Sew in all loose ends. Press (iron) the pieces carefully and sew the 13 stars in five rows, to the blue background (3 + 2 + 3 + 2 + 3). Place front and back pieces right sides together and sew together the sides. The top back piece should lie 2–3cm (¾–1¼in) above the bottom piece. Attach the blue buttons.

Classic diamonds

Finished size: 50 x 60cm (20 x 24in)

Materials
Zip 40cm (16in)

Yarn
Lerke from Dala Garn (merino wool/cotton)
200g (7oz) dark blue no. 5563
150g (5½oz) white no. 0020

4mm (size 6) needles

CO 276 sts with blue yarn on a circular needle and knit k129, p2, k129, p2 following the diagram. Place stitch markers before and after each purl section to help keep track of the front and back panels.

This work has pretty long leaps of yarn. It is therefore important to weave along the yarn on the back. Also make sure that you don't tighten the thread too much.

Continue until it measures approximately 50cm (20in).

Assembly:
Secure all loose ends and press (iron) the work carefully.
Sew the zip as shown in Good Advice.
Sew together the top and at the bottom sides with kitchener stitches.

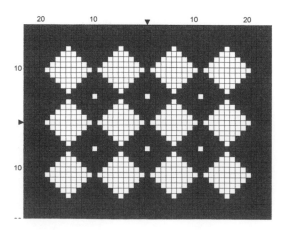

Stars and stripes

Materials
Zip 35cm (14in)

Yarn
PT Petunia from Rauma Ullvarefabrikk
(cotton)
250g (9oz) white no. 296
50g (1¾oz) blue no. 277
50g (1¾oz) red no. 256

3½mm (size 4) circular needle
3mm (size 3) crochet hook

Finished size: 45 x 45cm (18 x 18in)

Working in the round:
CO 180 sts on a circular needle. Knit k until
it measures approximately 40cm (16in)
and the pillow is almost square.

Crochet star:
Use blue yarn.
Round 1: Crochet 4 ch, make a ring
with 1 sl st in first ch, 1 ch.
Round 2: Crochet 6 sc in the ring,
finish with 1 sl st in first sc, 1 ch.
Round 3: 2 sc in each sc = 12 sc, finish
with 1 sl st in first sc, 1 ch.
Round 4: *1 sc, 1 ch (= small star loop),

1 sc in next st, 4 ch, 1 sc in the fourth ch from
the needle, 1 ch*, repeat from * to * (= 6 small
star loops) finish with 1 sl st in first sc.
Cut off the thread and pull through.
Crochet 17 stars in total.

Striped edge:
CO 6 sts with red yarn. Knit to end. When
you have finished the first row, tighten the
thread on the backside of the work and knit
a new row k without turning the work. Switch
to white yarn and do the same thing: Knit to
end, tighten the thread on the backside of the
work and start the next row from the right.
Continue with 2 red and 2 white rows until the
string measures approximately 160cm (63in).

Assembly:
Sew in all loose ends. Press (iron) the pieces
carefully. Sew the 17 blue stars onto the
white piece in 5 rows (3 + 4 + 3 + 4 + 3).
Add the zip as described in Good
Advice and sew together.
Sew the red and white string in a circle
using kitchener stitch. Run the string
around the pillow, pin and sew in place.

Sheepskin jacket revival

Much good leather is tucked away in Norwegian attics. As for me, I had an old sheepskin jacket hanging up from the 1970s. You can also find similar garments in second hand stores. It can be far cheaper than buying new leather.

Use a sharp knife and open out the seams to get pieces that lay flat. If it's possible, try to preserve and reuse details such as buttoning and pockets. Use a tape measure and an angled ruler, and consider how you can get the most from the different parts. Mark with a pencil before you cut.

For the brown pillow, I have used the largest pieces from the top part of the jacket. The back piece is made from the back of the jacket and the buttoning in the front is used as front piece. This avoids worrying about how to close the pillow. On this pillow, I lacked a little piece in one of the corners to make it 42 x 42cm (16½ x 16½in), including seam allowance. I therefore had to add more leather.

To sew leather is almost as easy as sewing wool and felt. You do not have to worry about the edges fraying. Place fur side to fur side; fastening with clothes pegs if necessary. Use a regular sharp needle or a small leather needle and buttonhole thread. Secure the thread and tack (baste) a little way inside the edge. If you're using a leather needle, make sure you don't cut the fabric.

Pull the fur out if you want it to show or push it in if you don't, before you sew. If you find it difficult to sew in a straight line, you can use masking tape to help you.

Star-spangled banner

Yarn
Lerke from Dale Garn (merino wool/wotton)
100g (3½oz) red no. 4018
50g (1½oz) white no. 0020
250g (9oz) blue no. 5563

4.5mm (size 7) needles

Finished size: 45 x 60cm (18 x 24in)

Front:
CO 100 sts with red yarn and knit k back and forth for 24 rows so that you get 12 rows of garter stitch. *Switch to white and knit 12 rows of garter, switch to red and knit 12 rows of garter*. Repeat from * to * 3 times, until you have 4 red and 3 white stripes. Switch to blue yarn. Knit 24 rows of garter before you cast (bind) off to 7 button holes: Knit k13, cast (bind) off the next 2 sts, *knit k10, cast (bind) off the next 2 sts*. Repeat from * to * 6 times, knit the last k13. Knit k13 back, *CO 2 sts, knit k10*. Repeat from * to * 6 times. CO 2 sts and finish with k13. Continue until you have 28 blue rows of garter before you cast (bind) off.

Back:
CO 100 sts with blue yarn and knit k back and forth until it is the same size as the front piece. Cast (bind) off.

Stars:
Sew with double thread. Secure the thread as shown in Good Advice and sew two large cross stitches on top of each other to form a star. The stitches do not have to be even, look neat, or be the same size. Scatter them randomly around the blue section of the pillow.

Assembly:
Sew in all loose ends.

Sew buttonhole stitches with double thread around the 7 holes, as described in Good Advice. Use matching blue buttons.

Place the two pieces wrong sides together and use a sturdy overstitch or crochet together with blue yarn. The buttons are sewn onto the wrong side of the back piece.

Nautical pillow

Materials
1 button

Yarn
PT Petunia from Rauma Ullvarefabrikk
(cotton)
350g (12oz) dark blue no. 277
50g (1¾oz) white no. 221

3.5mm (size 4) needles

Finished size: 54 x 54cm (21¼ x 21¼in)
(pillow 50 x 50cm (20 x 20in))

Blue back piece:
CO 110 sts with blue yarn. Knit k back and
forth for 10 rows until you have 5 rows of garter
stitch. Continue using garter stitches on the
5 outermost sts on each side of the work.
Stockinette stitch the middle 100 sts like this:
Forward: K.
Back: K5, p100, k5
until the work measures 52cm (20½in).
Finish with 10 rows k so you have 5 rows
of garter at the end. Cast (bind) off.

Blue front piece:
CO 110 sts with blue yarn. Knit k back and
forth for 10 rows until you have 5 rows of garter
stitch. Continue using garter stitches on the
5 outermost sts on each side of the work.
Stockinette stitch the middle 100 sts like this:
Forward: K.
Back: K5, p100, k5
Until the work measures 49.5cm (19½in). Knit
2 rows k making 1 garter row, knit the first 5 sts

k and place on a safety pin. Cast (bind) off the
next 100 by knitting 2 sts, slip the first st over the
second, knit another st k, slip the first st over
etc. until you have 5 sts left off the needle.

Cast (bind) off the last st like this:
Knit k2tog and k3 turn, knit k4 back turn, knit
k2tog and k2, knit k3 back turn, knit k2tog and
k1 turn, knit k2 back turn, knit ktog1 and finish.

Pick up the 5 sts on the left side of the work. Knit
from right to left and cast (bind) off the same way:
Knit k2tog and k3 turn, knit k4 back turn, knit
k2tog and k2, knit k3 back turn, knit k2tog and
k1 turn, knit k2 back turn, knit ktog1 and finish.

White front piece:
CO 3 sts with white yarn and knit the first row k.
Row 2: Knit k1, increase 1 by knitting 2 sts k
in next st and knit the remaining 2 sts k.
Row 3: Knit k1, increase 1 by knitting 2 sts k in
next st and knit the remaining 3 sts k. Continue
increasing 1 st in the beginning of each row until
you have 17 sts on the needle. Knit k1, increase 1 by
knitting 2 sts k in next st, knit k4, cast (bind) off the
next 4 for buttonhole by knitting k2, slip the back
st over the next etc. and finish with k6. You should
now have 7 sts on each side of the buttonhole.
Knit the next row k1, increase 1 by knitting 2 sts
k in next st, k5, CO 4 sts, and knit the last 7 sts k.
Continue increasing 1 st in the beginning of each
row until you have 103 sts on the needle. Switch
to blue yarn, and continue in the same way until
you have 110 sts. Then, continue until you have
5 blue rows of garter stitch. Cast (bind) off.

Embroider a blue stripe along the white edge. Chain
stitch in the sts that were increased on each row.

Sew buttonhole stitches around the
buttonhole (see Good Advice).

Assembly:
Press (iron) the three parts carefully. Place the white front piece
against the top edge of the blue back piece, wrong sides together.
Sew together with blue yarn inside the garter rows.

Then place the blue front piece against the blue back piece, right sides together
and edge-to-edge at the bottom. (The white top is folded over.) Sew the two
pieces together with blue yarn inside the garter edge. Sew together the blue
corners on the two front pieces, then make a seam of approximately 12cm (4½in)
in each side under the white fold, so that the opening is about 30cm (12in).

Finish by adding a gold button with an anchor or alternatively a blue button.

Love is...

Materials
30cm (12in) buttonhole elastic
17 small buttons

Yarn
PT Petunia from Rauma Ullvarafabrikk
(cotton)
200g (7oz) red no. 256
200g (7oz) white no. 221

3.5mm (size 4) needles

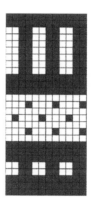

panel 1

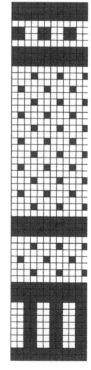

panel 3

Finished size: 50 x 50cm (20 x 20in)

CO 224 sts of red yarn on a circular needle.
Knit the same on the front and back side. Knit
the pattern from the diagram (right) 110 sts,
finish with p2. Repeat on the back piece.

Start with the panel 1, repeat 18 times in
width and finish with the 2 sts in border 1B.
Then knit panel 2 (see Two Pillows
in One for pattern).
Finish with panel 3, repeat 18 times in width and
finish with the 2 sts in panel 3. In some places
there will be pretty long leaps of yarn, it is therefore
important to twirl along the yarn in the back. It is
also important not to tighten the yarn too much.

Assembly:
Sew in all loose ends, press (iron) carefully
and use kitchener stitch in the top.
Sew on buttonhole elastic and buttons as
in Good Advice, and kitchener stitch the
remaining sts on each bottom side.

Denim details

Materials
An old duvet cover or two sheets, totalling about 90g (3¼oz) of fabric
1 worn out pair of jeans, adult size
Zip 50cm (20in)

7mm (size 10) needles

Finished size: 50 x 70cm (20 x 28in)

The rags should be 8–10mm (¼–½in) wide. Tear the rags lengthwise from the sheet. If you turn at the ends there will be fewer joins in the pillow, but then it is wise to hide the joins around the stitches around the "yarn".

When you have to join the ends, slope the ends of the rags about 10cm (4in) and lay them on top of each other.

CO 54 sts. Knit k back and forth until it measures 70cm (28in). Cast (bind) off.

Back:
Make the back piece out of something durable, such as an old pair of jeans. Cut off the legs but make sure that they measure at least 72cm (28½in) in length including the folded edge at the bottom. You may keep this as a characteristic detail. Cut up the insides of the legs and cut off the seams. Keep the seam on the outside. Press (iron) the fabric and cut them so they all have the same thread direction. Sew the zip as described in Good Advice.
Cut the back piece so that it measures 54 x 72cm (21¼ x 28½in) and overstitch around.

Assembly:
Sew in all loose ends. Use a crochet hook to push any undesirable joins to the backs of the work.

Cut out one of the back pockets of the jeans. Leave approximately 1cm (⅜in) of fabric outside the edge. Sew a heart with red thread; here it is done using a sewing machine. Remove the feed dog and lead the fabric back and forth. When you draw with paper and pencil, the pencil is the one moving, while when you embroider on a machine you have to move the fabric. Make it a little rough and sew a few hearts on top of each other.

Fold in the edges of the pocket, pin to the front piece and make a small overstitch. Fold in 2cm (¾in) along the edge on the back piece, except for the side that has the fold and seam. In the corners, fold in the tip first. Press (iron) then place front and back pieces right sides together, pin and sew a small overstitch by hand.

*If you can weave rag rugs, you can also knit them.
Tearing gives a softer appearance than if you cut. No
matter what you do, the result will be rough and sturdy.*

Blue cable cushion

Materials
Zip 35cm (14in)

Yarn
Lerke from Dale Garn (merino wool/cotton)
300g (10½oz) dark blue no. 6653

4.5mm (size 7) needles

Finished size: 45 x 45cm (18 x 18in)

CO 252 sts with blue yarn on a circular needle.
Row 1: *P2, k9, p2, tk1*.
Repeat from * to * 18 times.
Rows 2–3: As Row 1.

Row 4: *P2, k3, place the next 3 sts on a cn in front of the work while you knit the next 3 sts k. Then knit the 3 sts from the cn k, p2, tk1*. Repeat from * to * until the end of the row.
Rows 5–7: As row 1.
Row 8: *P2, place the next 3 sts on a cn behind the work while you knit the next 3 sts k. Then knit the 3 sts from the cn k, k3, p2, tk1*.

Repeat rows 1–8 until the work measures 45cm (18in).

Assembly:
Sew in all loose ends. Stretch out the work to correct the width (the cables contract it), and sew the zip by hand (see Good Advice). Sew the openings on each side of the zip and finally sew together the top.

WARMLY PRESENT

WANTED TO WEAVE – WAS BURNED ON THE FIRE

In the 1500s, Flemish weaving was very popular in upper class homes in large parts of Europe. It took some time for the trend to hit Norway, but at the end of the 1500s Anne Pedersdotter from Bergen ordered a frame from carpenter Giert that she wanted to use for this purpose. Anne was the widow of the priest and humanist Absalon Pederssøn Beyer. She was known as a strong and independent woman, but was also very argumentative and was therefore unpopular. There were rumours that she practiced witchcraft. When the carpenter and his wife did not want to give her the frame, she became mad. Soon after the carpenter's wife fell ill, Anne was accused of witchcraft.

In April 1590, Anne Pedersdotter was burned at the stake as a witch. One of the witnesses in the case against her was her own maid for 20 years. She said that Anne used her as her horse when she flew to witch gatherings at night.

Between 1579 and 1695, 860 women and men were accused of witchcraft in Norway. Anne Pedersdotter was one of the first to be executed. Most of the 307 that had to pay with their lives were women.

We think it was the northern German craftsmen who brought the art from Flanders to Norway. The technique, which has much in common with Kilim, spread from city to countryside, and in the 1700s Gudbransdalen became the centre of Flemish weaving in Norway. At this time weaving had become women's work.

Women primarily weaved tapestry but they also made cushions and pillows. There are hundreds of woven cushion covers from 1500s–1700s in Norwegian collections. Hynde were long pillows that were placed in the pews as seatbacks. Among the favorite subjects were the good and bad virgins, the Three Kings, and the feast of Herod. Stylized flowers, fruit, vases and animals were also popular. Some of the pillows were also made in half pile.

Lace knitting does not have to be as difficult as it looks. In the patterns given here, it's mostly about yarn over needle and knitting two stitches together. In addition, you need to be able to count to ten!

Leaf pattern

Materials
Grey-blue linen: 84 x 42cm (25½ x 16½in)
Zip 30cm (12in)

Yarn
UltraPima from Cascade Yarns (cotton)
100g (3½oz) sky blue no. 3727

3mm (size 3) needles

Finished size: 40 x 40cm (16 x 16in)

The stitch amount has to be a multiple of 10+1.
CO 81 sts.
Row 1: Purl all the sts.
Row 2: K3 *k2tog, yo1, k1, yo1, sl1, k1, psso, k5*.
Repeat from * to * until the end of the row.
Finish with k3 instead of k5.
Row 3 and all other odd numbered rows: Knit purl to end.
Row 4: K2, *k2tog, kq, yo1, k1, ktog1, k1, sl1, k1, psso, k3*.
Repeat from * to * until the end of the row.
Finish with k2 instead of 3.
Row 6: K1, *k2tog, k2, yo1, k1, yo1, k2, sl1, k1, psso, k1*.
Repeat from * to * until the end of the row.

Row 8: K2tog, *k3, yo1, k1 yo1, k3, sl1, k2tog, psso*. Repeat from * to * until the end of the row. Finish with k3, yo1, k1, yo1, k3, sl1, k1, psso.
Row 10: K1, *yo1, sl1, k1, psso, k5, k2tog, yo1, k1*.
Repeat from * to * until the end of the row.
Row 12: K1, *yo1, k1, sl1, k1, psso, k3, k2tog, k1, yo1, k1*.
Repeat from * to * until the end of the row.
Row 14: K1, *yo1, k2, sl1, k1, psso, k1, k2tog, k2, yo1, k1*.
Repeat from * to * until the end of the row.
Row 16: k1, *yo1, k3, sl1, k2tog, psso, k3, yo1, k1*.
Repeat from * to * until the end of the row.
Repeat rows 1 to 16 until the work is square.
(It should be approximately 40cm (16in) each way.)

Assembly:
Sew in all loose ends and overstich around the fabric. Place the fabric with the narrow end towards you and sketch up a square of 40 x 40cm (16 x 16in), 32cm (12¾in) from the edge. Place the lace on top of the fabric. Pin the edges and make a small overstitch around the work. Press (iron) the work from the backside.

Place the linen fabric right sides together and sew together approximately 5cm (2in) on each side. Press the seams apart before you sew the zip as described in Good Advice.

Reverse the work again so it has right sides together and sew a seam on each side.

Shell pattern

Materials
Grey-blue linen: 85 x 42cm (35½ x 16½in)
Zip 30cm (12in)

Yarn
UltraPima from Cascade Yarns (cotton)
100g (3½oz) sky blue no. 3727

4mm (size 6) needles

Finished size: 40 x 40cm (16 x 16in)

This pattern is a little more challenging than the Leaf Pattern because the lace design is worked on the R.S and W.S rows.

The st number must be a multiple of 6+2.
CO 80 sts and work 1 row purl.
Row 1: K1, *k4, k2tog, yo*.
Repeat until the end of the needle, finish with k1.
Row 2: P1, *p2, p2tog, p2, yo*.
Repeat until the end of the needle, finish with p1.
Row 3: K1, *k2, k2tog, k2, yo*.
Repeat until the end of the needle, finish with k1.
Row 4: P1, *yo, p3, p2tog, p1*.
Repeat until the end of the needle, finish with p1.
Row 5: K1, *k2tog, k4, yo*.
Repeat until the end of the needle, finish with k1.

Row 6: P2, *p4, yo, p2tog*.
Repeat until the end of the needle.
Row 7: K1, *k1, yo, k3, k2tog*.
Repeat until the end of the needle, finish with k1.
Row 8: P1, *p2tog, p2, yo, p2*.
Repeat until the end of the needle, finish with p1.
Row 9: K1, *k3, yo, k1, k2tog*.
Repeat until the end of the needle, finish with k1.
Row 10: P1, *p2tog, yo, p4*.
Repeat until the end of the needle, finish with p1.

Repeat 1 to 10 until the work is square (should measure about 40cm (16in) in each direction).

Assembly:
Sew in all loose ends and overstitch around the fabric. Place the narrow end of the fabric towards you and sketch a square measuring 40 x 40cm (16 x 16in), 32cm (12½in) from the edge. Place the knitted lace on the fabric. Pin around the edge and make a small overstitch. Press (iron) from the back of the work.

Place the linen fabrics right sides together with edges together, and sew together approximately 5cm (2in) on each side. Press the seams apart before you sew the zip as described in Good Advice.

Reverse the work again so you have the right sides together and sew a seam on each side.

Sea foam blanket

Yarn
Allino cottolin from BC garn (linen/cotton)
250g (9oz) turquoise no. 33
200g (7oz) dark blue no. 32
800g (1lb 12oz) blue no. 30
400g (14oz) dark grey no. 07
400g (14oz) light grey no. 06
200g (7oz) purple no. 11
Cotton baby from Gepard (cotton)
200g (7oz) spring green no. 109

6mm (size 10) needles

Finished size: approximately
1.7 x 2m (1.8½ x 2yds)

The whole blanket is knitted consistently
with two threads in the same colour.
CO 242 sts of turquoise yarn.
Row 1: Knit k (this will be the
backside of the blanket)
Row 2: K.
Row 3: P.
Row 4: K.
Row 5: P.

Row 6: *Tk2tog, tk2tog, yo1, k1,
yo1, k1, yo1, k1, yo1, k2tog, k2tog*.
Repeat the 11 sts to the end of the row.
Row 7: K.
**Switch to dark blue yarn and
repeat rows 4–7 once.
Switch to blue yarn and repeat twice.
Switch to dark grey yarn and repeat twice.
Switch to purple yarn and repeat once.
Switch to blue yarn and repeat once.
Switch to spring green yarn and repeat once.
Switch to light grey yarn and repeat twice.
Switch to blue yarn and repeat once.
Switch to turquoise and repeat once.**
Continue making stripes in this way from
** to ** until the blanket is about 2m (2yds)
or your desired length, and cast (bind) off.
Every stripe will measure about 24cm (9½in).

Assembly:
Sew in all loose ends.

Autumn plum

Materials
7 buttons

Yarn
PT Petunia from Rauma Ullvarefabrikk
(cotton)
150g (5½oz) grey no. 293 (colour A)
100g (3½oz) purple no. 260 (colour B)
50g (1¾oz) pink no. 200 (colour C)
50g (1¾oz) light green no. 214 (colour D)
150g (5½oz) light blue no. 270 (colour E)

3.5mm (size 4) crochet hooks

Square 1: C, C, C, A, D, B, A.
Square 2: E, E, E, E, E, B, A.
Square 3: A, A, A, C, A, E, B.
Square 4: B, B, B, C, A, C, A.
Square 5: C, C, C, B, C, A, B.
Square 6: B, B, B, E, B, C, A.
Square 7: B, B, B, C, B, D, A.
Square 8: B, B, B, B, B, C, A.
Square 9: C, C, C, B, A, C, A.
Square 10: A, A, A, C, A, B, A.
Square 11: D, D, D, D, D, B, A.
Square 12: A, A, A, B, A, C, B.
Square 13: C, C, C, C, C, B, A.
Square 14: A, A, A, C, B, A, B.
Square 15: B, B, B, A, C, B, A.
Square 16: B, B, D, A, B, C, A.

Finished size: 40 x 40cm (16 x 16in)

Granny squares:
Start with 4 ch and make into a ring with 1 sl st.
Round 2: Crochet 12 sc into the ring.
Round 3: Crochet 2 dc in each sc.
Round 4: Crochet 2 dc and 1 ch.
Repeat until the end of the row.
Round 5: Crochet 3 dc around every ch loop
and 1 ch in-between until the end of the row.
Round 6: *Crochet 3 dc around every ch
loop and 1 ch in-between 3 times. Crochet
3 ch and 3 new dc in the same ch*.
Repeat from * to * until the end
of the row, that is 4 times.
The circle is now a square.
Round 7: Crochet 3 dc around every ch curve and
1 ch in-between on the sides. In the corners crochet
3 dc, 3 ch and 3 new dc in the same ch loop.
You will need 16 granny squares in total. The colours
are spread out from inside to outside, like this:

Back piece, bottom part:
Crochet 78 ch in light blue yarn, turn, skip
1 st and crochet 77 sc back. Crochet dc,
but start with 2 ch on each row that makes
first dc before you yo and continue.
Continue until the work measures
36cm (14¼in). Finish with 1 row sc.

Back piece, top part:
Crochet 78 ch in light blue yarn, turn, skip
1 st and crochet 77 sc back. Crochet dc,
but start with 2 ch on each row that makes
first dc before you yo and continue.
Continue until the work measures 9cm (3½in).
Switch to grey yarn and crochet 1 row dc and
1 row sc. Crochet 1 ch extra when you turn.
Crochet buttonhole like this: 7 sc, *3 ch,
skip 3 sc and continue with 7 sc*. Repeat
from * to * until the end of the row.
Next row: 1 ch when you turn, 7 sc,
3 cs around the ch loop, 7 sc.
Repeat from * to * until the end of the row.

Finish with 1 row of sl st and 1 row sc.

Assembly:

Secure all loose ends and press (iron) the parts gently. Crochet the squares together on the backside by placing the squares right sides together and crochet 2 sc in each ch loop and 2 ch in-between. Crochet loosely so that the thread doesn't tighten when you turn (see Good Advice) When all the 16 squares are crocheted together, crochet 1 row around the entire work with grey yarn.

The top part of the back piece is sewn above the bottom part so that it forms a square. Sew on the buttons.

Place the front and back pieces wrong sides together and crochet the two parts together with sc in light blue yarn. Do not tighten the thread. Reverse the work.

13	14	15	16
9	10	11	12
5	6	7	8
1	2	3	4

Shooting star

Materials
5 buttons

Yarn
Easy from SandnesGarn (merino wool)
250g (9oz) dark purple no. 4855
100g (3½oz) light purple no. 4853

7mm (size 10) needles

Finished size: 40 x 40cm (16 x 16in)

CO 130 sts on a circular needle
with dark purple yarn.
Row 1: Knit k1, p1 until the end of the row.
Row 2: Knit p1, k1 until the end of the row.
Continue with k64, p1, k64 and
p1 until the work is done.
Row 3–6: Knit with dark purple yarn.
Row 7–20: *Knit k5 with dark purple yarn, follow
the diagram (black square is light purple yarn)
3 times and then the next 13 sts in the diagram.
Finish with k5 in dark purple yarn and
p1 (yo around the light yarn)*.
Repeat from * to * so that the back side is the same.
Repeat rows 3–20 so that you get 4 rows of stars.
Finish with 4 rows of dark yarn and cast (bind) off.

Assembly:
Sew in all loose ends and press (iron) the
work carefully. Sew together the top and
approximately 7cm (2¾in) on each side with
kitchener stitches. Sew loops as described in
Good Advice then sew the buttons in place.

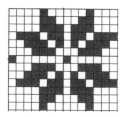

To knit or not to knit

Materials
6 buttons

Yarn
Petunia from Rauma Ullvarefabrikk (cotton)
Light green no. 247
Blue no. 274
Light grey no. 270
Plum no. 260

3.5mm (size 4) needles

Finished size: 40 x 40cm (16 x 16in)

CO 184 sts on a circular needle with light green yarn and knit k. Follow the diagram below on both front- and backsides. When you have finished the first border up until the plum line, repeat the pattern before you continue with border 2.

Assembly:
Sew in all loose ends.
Kitchener stitch the top and 10cm (4in) on each side at the bottom. Sew loops as described in Good Advice and sew buttons in place.

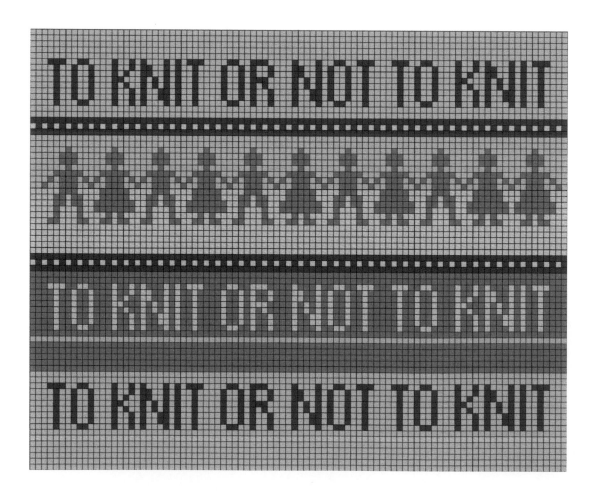

Bluebirds

The inspiration for this pillow is from an old mitten pattern where the large birds are on the top of the mitten and the small birds are used on the thumb.

Materials
7 buttons

Yarn
Petunia from Rauma Ullvarefabrikk (cotton)
200g (7oz) lime green no. 216
100g (3½oz) blue no. 275
100g (3½oz) turquoise no. 274
50g (1¾oz) light green no. 247

3.5mm (size 4) needles

Finished size: 50 x 50cm (20 x 20in)

CO 234 sts with green yarn.

Rounds 1–4: Knit 116 sts from diagram, p1, k 116 sts from diagram, p1. Place stitch markers before and after each purl section to help keep track of front and back panels.

Next round: *Starting at row 29 of diagram work across first 116 sts, p1, repeat from * to end.

Continue working from diagram until row 74 is completed. Weave ends in across the back of work, making sure you don't pull or tighten the yarn.

Work rows 43–60 from diagram, then rows 29–44. Then work rows 1–10 of diagram.

Next round: k116, p1, k116, p1

Repeat last round 3 more times.

Assembly:
Sew in all loose ends and press (iron) the work carefully.
Sew on the buttons as described in Good Advice and sew together on the top and bottom sides using kitchener stitches.

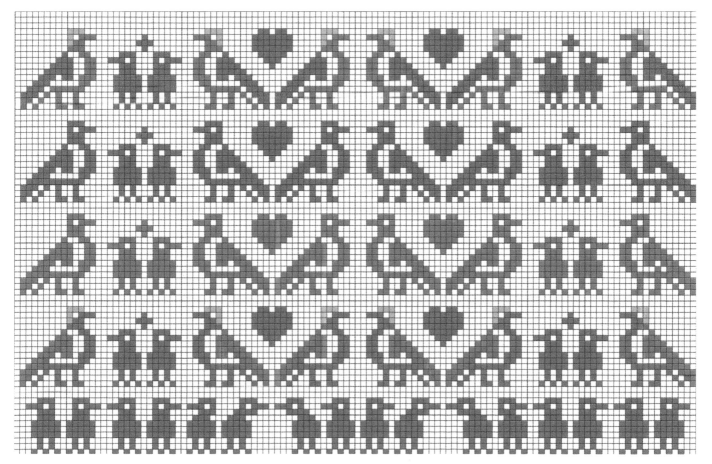

It is perfectly fine to knit two pillows at the same time – sometimes it can be pretty smart.

Two pillows in one

Materials
Fabric for backside, for example purple velvet, 60 x 52cm (24 x 20¾in) twice.

Yarn
Zara from Filatura Di Crosa (merino wool)
200g (7oz) dark purple no. 1494
150g (5½oz) grey no. 1494

3.5mm (size 4) needles

Finished size: 30 x 50cm (12 x 20in)

CO 236 sts with purple yarn and knit p4, k110, p8, k110 and p4. Continue with the pattern from diagram 1 until it measures 12cm (4¾in), and at the same time knit p8 on each side to separate the two patterns. Knit diagram 2 and then continue with diagram 1 until the work measures 29cm (11½in). Finish with 4 rows of purple yarn and cast (bind) off.

Cable edge:
CO 12 sts in purple (grey) yarn.
Knit k2, p8, k2.
*Knit p2, k8, p2 and k2, p8, k2 back 4 times.
Knit p2, place 4 sts on cn behind the work, knit k4, then the 4 sts on the cn k, p2.
Knit k2, p8, k2 back*. Repeat from * to * until the cable measures 1.6m (1.7½yds).

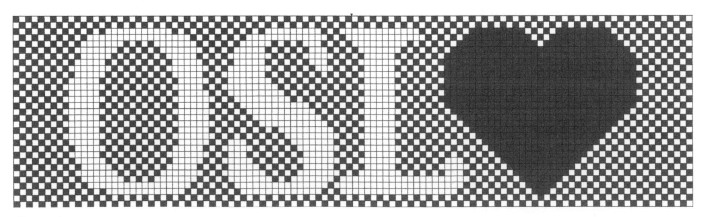

diagram 1

Assembly:

Sew in all loose ends.

On the purl stitches on each side, machine stitch two seams of zigzag stitch before you cut the two pieces apart. Press (iron) the work carefully. Each piece should measure 30.5 x 50.5cm (12¼ x 20¼in).

Find suitable fabric for the back panel and cut out two pieces measuring 62 x 62cm (24½ x 24½in) – one for each pillow. Overstitch around the fabric with a machine. Place the wrong side of the knitted work on the right side of the fabric, about 10cm (4in) from the back piece's bottom edge, pin and sew together. Make sure the work doesn't stretch. Place the velvet and the work right sides together

with the edges towards each other, and sew together 10cm (4in) on each side. Press (iron) the seams apart before you sew in the zip (see Good Advice). Press (iron) the work carefully and sew the sides together from the right side.

Sew the cable to a circle and attach with pins. Sew with small stitches on the front side first and then on the backside so that you hide the seam that keeps the front- and backsides together. Do the same with pillow 2, making the cable from grey yarn this time.

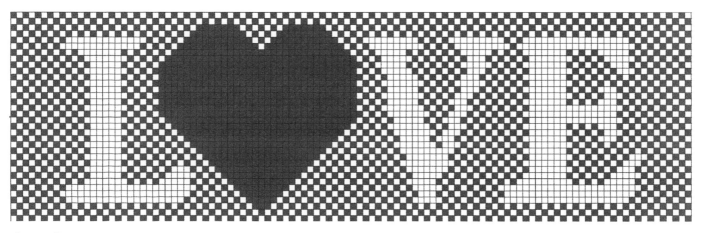

diagram 2

IN THE ROSE GARDEN

THE NEEDLE – SMALL BUT SIGNIFICANT

At the end of the 1800s there was a Danish pastor's wife living in Aurdal in Valdres. She brought eight pins from her childhood home. It is said that she counted the pins every night before she went to bed to make sure that none of them were missing.

Pins were forged one-by-one by hand. As the import of costly fabrics accelerated in the 1400s, the need for pins to hold the fabrics together increased. The French pins had a reputation for being the best because they were smooth and did not fray the fabric. When the English began to make brass pins in the 1600s, these were the ones to have. Attempts were made to start their own pin industry in the US in the 1700s, but even President Washington had to order his pins from England. It was not until 1824, when the American Lemul Wellmann patented a machine that could make pins in one operation, that European producers had competition. Wellmann's pins had heads that prevented them falling off – a huge improvement.

The sewing needle has never been regarded as an important tool but it was just as significant as the spear in the prehistoric times. Sewing needles probably date back to more than 10,000 years ago. Pins were essential to make the garments that kept the bodies warm and dry during the ice age. It was not until the Iron Age, about 1250 BC, that they started to make needles from iron. And when the Arabs conquered Spain in 600 AD, they brought with them the art of forging steel. Steel needles did not bend as easily.

In the early 1800s, needles were made partly mechanically. Strands of steel were cut, annealed and sharpened at both ends. The needles were turned flat in the middle and two eyes were made. They were then split in half, the eyes were smoothed and the heads rounded. They had to be hardened, polished, washed, dried and eventually wrapped in silver paper with black paper on the outside to prevent rusting. In the colonies, the climate was in some places so humid that they couldn't use the regular needles. Here they had to forge needles from gold or silver so that they wouldn't rust.

Home tweet home

Materials
Turquoise wool fabric 54 x 74cm (21¼ x 29in) for front piece and 54 x 54cm (21¼ x 21¼in) for back piece. Since the fabric is relatively thick, these measurements are for a 2cm (¾in) seam allowance and 20cm (8in) fold
Purple felt

Yarn
Use some leftover yarn for the embroidery; you only need a few metres of each colour. Here we've used Falk from Dale Garn (wool)
Orange no. 3609
Light green no. 8817
Dale baby wool
Pink no. 4516

Small heart:
Falk from Dale Garn
50g (1¾in) red no. 4018 or red leftover yarn

Lace edge:
Falk from Dale Garn (wool)
50g (1¾in) purple no. 5036 or purple leftover yarn

3mm or 3.5mm (size 3 or 4) needles

Finished size: 50 x 50cm (20 x 20in)

Small red heart:
CO 3 sts and knit 1 row k. Continue k as you increase 1 st on each side of the central st every third row. Repeat until you have 51 sts on the needle. Knit 27 sts. Cast (bind) off the middle st by passing the 26th st over the 27th. Continue until the end of the row.

Leave the stitches on the right side of the work on the needle while you continue with the left part. *Start by knitting the first 2 sts to one, knit to the end of the needle. Repeat back. Then knit back and forth without casting (binding) off*. Repeat from * to * 3 times.
Knit the first 2 sts to one, knit to the end of the needle. Repeat back.
Repeat from * to * 4 times.
Cast (bind) off the last 11 sts.
Knit the right side of the work in the same way.

Assembly and embroidery:
All the embroidery is done by hand without sketching. It gives the pillow a naïve appearance, as is often seen in old woollen embroidery. The simple and less perfect approach creates charm, so don't be afraid to try it. If you are not happy, simply undo a couple of stitches and try again.

Reverse the red heart in the centre of the front piece and backstitch or tack (baste) around the edge with red yarn. Cut out two birds from purple felt and place them on each side of the heart, tack (baste) around the edge with green yarn. Tie a French knot to use as the eye and give it three small tail feathers. The legs are sewn with outline stitches.

The spirals that spread out of the top of the heart are made with outline stitches in orange yarn. Decorate around the heart with French knots using pink yarn. Finish with a small flower in loop stitch.

The text is sewn with outline stitch in green yarn. It should be centred, so start with the middle E in TWEET, sewing this right underneath the heart. Continue with the letters on the right side first. Press (iron) the work carefully on the back.

Place front and back pieces right sides together and sew the pillow with fold (see Good Advice).

Lace edge:
Use purple yarn to chain stitch the seam around the pillow and along the fold at the bottom of the front piece.
Row 1: Crochet 1 sc in the first chain stitch, 3 ch, 1 sc in the third chain stitch, 3 ch, 1 sc in the fifth chain stitch, 3 ch, etc. Continue with 1 ch every other chain stitch until you get to the first corner. Then you crochet 3 sc in the corner stitch. Continue the same way all the way around.
Row 2: Crochet 1 sc, 3 ch and 1 sc in each ch loop the whole way around. Secure the thread.

Tassel pillow

Yarn
PT3 from Rauma Ullvarefabrikk (wool)
100g (3½oz) red no. 7018
100g (3½oz) pink no. 7054

6mm (size 10) needles

Finished size: 40 x 40cm (16 x 16in)

CO 3 sts with pink yarn and knit to end.
Row 2: K1, M1 by picking up the strand in between sts with RHN, slip onto LHN and knit back, knit to end.
Row 3: As row 2.

Continue increasing by 1 in the beginning of every row until the width is 40cm (16in). Then you should have about 87 sts on the needle. Switch to red yarn and knit 1 row k without increasing. Then knit k1, k2tog and the rest of the sts on the needle k. Continue to cast (bind) off 1 st at the beginning of each row by knitting k1 and k2tog in this way until you have 3 sts left on the needle. Cast (bind) off.

Knit the back piece the same way.

Assembly:
Place the two pieces wrong sides together so that the pink edge is against the red and vice versa. Overstitch around on three sides and approximately 5cm (2in) on the bottom side. Sew 6 buttonhole loops (see Good Advice) and sew on the buttons.

Make four tassels from pink yarn and sew one to each corner.

Pink borders

Finished size: 60 x 60cm (24 x 24in)

Materials
Zip 50cm (20in)

Yarn
Mandarin Petit from SandnesGarn (cotton)
200g (7oz) pink no. 4505
200g (7oz) dark pink no. 4518
100g (3½oz) red no. 4418
50g (1¾oz) orange no. 2708
50g (1¾oz) turquoise no. 6705

Safran from Garnstudio (cotton)
100g (3½oz) pistachio green no. 31
50g (1¾oz) light pink no. 1
50g (1¾oz) shaded yarn no. 32 (can be replaced by turquoise Mandarin Petit)

3mm (size 3) needles

CO 336 sts with light pink yarn on a circular needle.

Work rounds 1–31 from the first border diagram in the Patterns section, repeating the 12 sts border pattern 28 times.

Repeat this process working from each border diagram until all have been completed. Weave ends in across the back of work, also make sure you don't pull or tighten the yarn.

Assembly:
Sew in all loose ends. Sew in the zip (see Good Advice). Sew together at the top and on the sides of the bottom.

Red rose pillow

Materials
Red wool fabric for the back piece,
approximately 42 x 42cm (16½ x 16½in)

Yarn
Sterk from Du Store Alpakka
(alpaca/merino wool/nylon)
200g (7oz) red no. 094

3.5mm (size 4) crochet hooks

Finished work: 40cm (16in) in diameter

Base:
Crochet 5 ch and make a ring with
1 sl st. Crochet two ch and continue
with dc around the ring, total 12.
Place a stitch holder that marks
where the row begins and ends.
Continue by crocheting dc in a thread from
the backside of the work, so that the sts
from the last row are on the front side of the
work as a continuous line of sl st. Continue
in the same direction the whole time.
Row 2: Crochet 1 sc, then 1 dc.
Continue with 2 dc in each st, so
that you get 24 sts in total.
Row 3: Crochet *2 dc in the first st and
1 dc in the next st*.
Repeat until the end of the row.
Move the stitch holder as you move outwards.
Row 4: Continue with *1 dc into next
2 sts, then 2 dc in the next st*.
Repeat until the end of the row.
In every new row, increase the amount of dc
that you crochet individually with 1 dc.
Row 5: *1 dc into next 3 sts,
then 2 dc in next st*.
Row 6: *1 dc into next 4 sts,
then 2 dc in next st*.

Row 7: *1 dc into next 5 sts,
then 2 dc in next st*.
Row 8: *1 dc into next 6 sts, then 2 dc in next st*.
Row 9: *1 dc into next 7 sts, then 2 dc in next st*.
Row 10: *1 dc into next 8 sts, then 2 dc in next st*.
Row 11: *1 dc into next 9 sts, then 2 dc in next st*.
Row 12: *1 dc into next 10 sts, then 2 dc in next st*.
Row 13: *1 dc into next 11 sts, then 2 dc in next st*.
Row 14: *1 dc into next 13 sts, then 2 dc in next st*.
Row 15: *1 dc into next 15 sts, then 2 dc in next st *
Row 16: *1 dc into next 17 sts, then 2 dc in next st *.
Row 17: *1 dc into next 19 sts, then 2 dc in next st*.
Row 18: *1 dc into next 25 sts, then 2 dc in next st*.
Row 19: *1 dc into next 30 sts, then 2 dc in next st*.
Row 20: *1 dc into next 35 sts, then 2 dc in next st*.
Continue this way until it measures
42cm (16½in) in diameter.

Rose spiral:
Secure the thread in the centre of the circle
and crochet 1 sc in the first st on the front
side of the work. Continue with 2 dc in each
st until you have crocheted 9 rows.

Crochet 1 dc in the first st and 2 in the next
3 rows, before you go back to 2 dc in each
st for 1 row. Repeat these 4 rows before
you crochet 2 dc in each st until you are
one row from the edge. End with 1 sc.

Assembly:
Alternatively you could crochet the back
piece the same way that you made the base
(you would need 100g (3½oz) extra yarn).

Here we have used red wool fabric. Cut out
a circle with a 42cm (16½in) diameter. Use a
sewing machine to overstitch around the fabric.

Sew in all loose ends.

Place front and back pieces right sides together
and sew around by hand or on the machine. Leave

an opening of about 20cm (8in). Reverse the work and fill with a round pillow. If necessary, cut out a small red circle that is placed between the pillow and the crochet so that the pillow is not visible through the crochet. Stitch up the opening using small stitches.

In this work we started by making a base and then the rose petals – if we can call them that – are crocheted to the base as an eternity spiral.

The @ sign was unknown to my great-grandmothers. It is probably not likely that they would have chosen to embroider SOFAGRIS (couch potato in Norwegian) on a pillow either! The shape and detail of the letters is from a lost time. If you prefer, you could replace this with another expression, e.g. Carpe Diem (seize the day). There are numerous alphabet patterns to choose from; just put together the letters that you need. A small heart at one or both ends can fill space if the pattern does not fill the entire width of the cushion.

Couch potato cushion

Materials
White cotton canvas for embroidery, 9 threads per cm, approximately 8 x 42cm (3¼ x 16¾in)
White linen, 18 x 42cm (7 x 16½) and 41 x 42cm (16¼ x 16½in) for front piece, and 13 x 42cm (5¼ x 21¾in) and 53 x 42cm (21¾ x 16¾in) for the back piece
Zip 35cm (14in)

Yarn
Mouliné fine yarn:
1 skein red no. 666
1 skein pink no. 62

Finished size: 40 x 60cm (16 x 24in)

Find the centre of the cotton fabric and follow the diagram. Sew cross stitches over 2 x 2 threads.

Assembly:
Pull out two threads under and two threads over the red cross stitch rows. You should have two threads in-between.
Fold the linen following the thread direction, place the embroidery underneath, pin and sew the two layers together.

Sew the zip to the back piece (see Good Advice). Place the front and back pieces right sides together, pin and sew around. Cut off excess fabric in the corners press (iron) the seams apart and reverse the work.

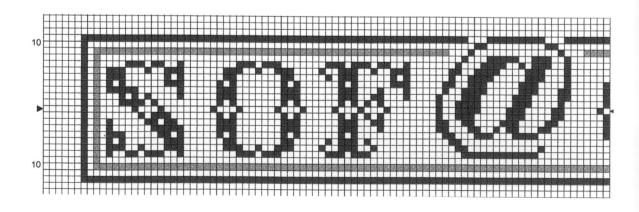

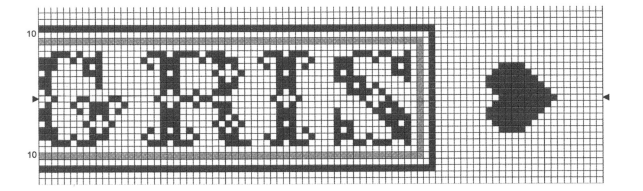

Red and pink cable blanket

Yarn
PT3 from Rauma Ullvarefabrikk (wool)
700g (1lb 9oz) red no. 7018
850g (1 lb 14oz) pink no. 7054

If you want to make the blanket bigger and use it e.g. as a bedspread, you need to allow more yarn. 50g (1¾oz) red is enough for about 12cm (4¾in). 50g (1¾oz) pink is enough for about 11cm (4½in).

Materials
6mm (size 10) needles
Minimum 80cm (32in) long

Finished size: 1.1 x 1.7m (1¼ x 2yds)

CO 240 sts of red yarn. Knit moss stitch (k1, p1 first row, opposite back) for 5cm (2in). Continue with moss stitch on the sides and cables in pink and red.

NB: There are two things you will need to remember when working this design:
a) It is important that you don't tighten the thread too much on the back. If you do, the blanket will be very dense and narrow. Place a finger or two underneath the thread when you start a new colour.
b) The second challenge begins in the second row when you have to start the first cable. To

get a nice and even edge between the pink moss stitch and the first red cable, you have to twist the red and pink yarn around one another before you continue knitting. You must do this on every row no matter if you knit k or p.

Cable Pattern:
Row 1: 8 sts moss stitch in pink, *k8 and p1 in red, k8 and p1 in pink*. Repeat from * to * 12 times. K8 in red, finish with 8 sts in moss stitch.
Row 2: 8 sts moss stitch in pink, p8 in red, *k1 and p8 in pink, k1 and p8 in red*. Repeat from * to * 12 times. Finish with 8 sts moss stitch. Repeat these 2 rows 5 more times.
Row 13: 8 sts moss stitch in pink. *Place the first 4 sts in red on a cn behind the work, knit k4 before you knit the 4 on the cn k and p1 in red. Switch to pink yarn. Place 4 sts on a cn, knit k4 before you knit the 4 sts on the cn k and p1. Repeat from * to * 12 times. Switch back to red yarn. Place 4 sts on a cn, knit k4 before you knit the 4 sts on the cn k. Finish with 8 sts moss stitch.
Row 13: Repeat Row 2.
Continue by repeating the pattern but from now on rows 1 and 2 should only be repeated 5 times before you twist the cables. When the blanket measures approximately 1.65m (1¾yds), finish with 5cm (2in) of pink moss stitch before you cast (bind) off.

Hot pink cables

Materials
Cotton fabric for back piece,
43 x 52cm (17 x 20¾in) and
13 x 52cm (5 x 20¾in)
Zip, 30cm (12in)
45cm (18in) velvet ribbon,
approximately 8mm (¼in) wide

Yarn
PT Petunia from Rauma
Ullvarefabrikk (cotton)
100g (3½oz) orange no. 245
150g (5oz) pink no. 722

3.5mm (size 4) needles

Finished size: 50 x 50cm (20 x 20in)/
40 x 40cm (16 x 16in)

Diamond pattern:

To get the diagonals of k st to tilt to the right or left, the sts have to switch places. Do this by using a cn.

SR means switch right; place 1 st on cn behind the work and knit the next 2 sts on the left needle k before you knit the sts on the cn p. This is 3 sts.

SL means switch left; place 2 sts onto the cn in front of the work and knit 1 st on the left needle p. Knit the 2 sts on the cn k. This is 3 sts.

CO 110 sts with orange yarn and knit k back. Continue knitting the base p on the right side and k on the wrong side in orange yarn. The cables are knitted k on right side and p on wrong side in pink yarn.

Row 1 (right side): P4, SR, SL, *p6, SR, SL*. Repeat from * to * 8 times. The last 4 sts on the needle are knitted p.

Row 2: K4, p2, k2, p2, *k6, p2, k2, p2*. Repeat from * to * until you have 4 sts left. These are knitted k.

Row 3: P3, SR, p2, SL, *p4, SR, p2, SL*. Repeat from * to * until you have 3 sts left on the needle. These are knitted p.

Row 4: K3, p2, *k4, p2*. Repeat from * to * until you have 3 sts left on the needle. These are knitted k.

Row 5: *P2, SR, p4, SL*. Repeat from * to * until you have 2 sts left on the needle. These are knitted k.

Row 6: K2, p2, k6, *p2, k2, p2, k6*. Repeat from * to * until you have 4 sts left on the needle. These are knitted p2 and k2.

Row 7: P1, *SR, p6, SL*. Repeat from * to * until you have 1 st left on the needle. This is knitted p.

Row 8: K1, p2, k8, *p4, k8*. Repeat from * to * until you have 3 sts left on the needle. These are knitted p2, k1.

Row 9: P1, k2, p8*. Place 2 sts on cn behind the work, knit 2 sts k and then the 2 on the cn k, p8*. Repeat from * to * until you have 3 sts left on the needle. These are knitted k2, p1.

Row 10: Repeat Row 8.

Row 11: P1, *SL, p6, SR*. Repeat from * to * until you have 1 st left on the needle. This is knitted p.

Row 12: Repeat Row 6.

Row 13: *P2, SL, p4, SR*. Repeat from * to * until you have 2 sts left on the needle. These are knitted p.

Row 14: Repeat Row 4.

Row 15: P3, SL, p2, SR, *p4, SL, p2, SR*. Repeat from * to * until you have 3 sts left on the needle. These are knitted p.

Row 16: Repeat Row 2.

Row 17: P4, SL, SR, *p6, SL, SR*. Repeat from * to * until you have 4 sts left on the needle. These are knitted p.

Row 18: K5, p4, *k8, p4*. Repeat from * to * until you have 5 sts left on the needle. These are knitted k.

Row 19: P5, place 2 sts on cn behind the work, knit 2 sts k and then the 2 on the cn k, *p8, 2 sts on cn behind the work, knit 2 sts k and then knit 2 on the cn k*. Repeat from * to * until you have 5 sts left on the needle. These are knitted p.

Row 20: Repeat Row 18.
Repeat these 20 rows 5 times and cast (bind) off.

Pink edge:
CO 356 sts with pink yarn on a circular needle. Knit the first row without increasing. Start the next row with *yo1, k89, yo1, k1*. Repeat from * to * until the end of the row. In this way you increase with 2 sts in each corner. Continue increasing in the same way until the work measures approximately 5cm (2in) and you have 115 sts on each long side. Knit 1 row p, but the 4 corner sts are knitted k. Knit *k2tog, k113, p2. ktog, k1*. Repeat from * to * until the end of the row. In this way you decrease the sts around in each corner by 2 sts. Continue casting (binding) off this way until the back part is approximately 5cm (2in).

Assembly:
Press (iron) the work gently on the wrong side.
Sew the zip in on the back piece (see Good Advice).
Place the back and front pieces wrong sides together and sew around the edge.
Sew the pink edge to the front piece by hand, fold around the edge and sew it to the backside.
Sew on a red ribbon by hand, above the seam between the front piece and the pink edge.

The technique that is used here makes it possible to use almost any kind of leftover yarn.

Bright and beautiful

Materials
4 buttons

Yarn
50g (1¾oz) thin alpaca from Du Store Alpakka, red no. 179
Various yarn in shades of orange, red, pink and purple (wool and alpaca)

4.5mm or 5mm (sizes 7 or 8) needles

Finished size: 30 x 40cm (12 x 16in)

Always knit with two or three threads that have approximately the same thickness. Adjust the needle size to suit the thickness of the yarn. When you switch yarn, only switch one thread at a time. This way you will get even and smooth

transitions in the colour and thickness of the yarn. Start with, for example, two threads of red, then switch one red to purple and knit one row, continue one row of purple but switch the red to orange, etc.

CO 45 sts with two threads of red yarn and knit k on the front side and k5, p5, k5, p5, k5, p5, k5, p5, k5 back 6 times in total. Knit k on the front side and k6, p3, k6, p3, k6, etc. back. Then k on the front side and k7, p1, k7, p1, k7, etc. back.
Continue knitting k both ways until the work measures 86cm (34in), while you switch yarn as described above. Use the red yarn regularly.

Assembly:
Secure all loose ends. Fold the striped work in half and sew the sides. Position the pillow. Place four decorative buttons on the red top before you sew them onto the pillow with small stitches.

Red heart pillow

CO 3 sts of red yarn and work 1 row knit.
Continue knitting k while you increase by 1 st on
each side of the central stitch every third row.
Repeat until you have 111 sts on the needle.
Knit 57 sts. Cast (bind) off the central sts by
passing the 56th st over the 57th. Continue
until the end of the needle. Leave the sts on
the right side of the work on the needle while
you continue with the left side of the work.
*Start by knitting the first 2 sts to 1, knit to the end
of the needle. Repeat back. Knit back and forth
without decreasing*. Repeat from * to * 6 times.
Knit the first 2 st to 1, knit to the end
of the needle. Repeat back.
*Cast (bind) off the first 5 sts, knit to the end of
the needle. Repeat back*. Repeat 4 times.
Cast (bind) off the last 8 st. Knit the right
side of the work in the same way.

Cable edge:
CO 16 sts with pink yarn.
Row 1: Knit k2, p12, k2. (This is on the backside.)
Row 2: Knit p2, k12, p2.
Repeat Rows 1 and 3 three times in total.
Row 7: Knit p2, place the next 3 sts on a cn
behind the work, knit k3, knit the 3 from the
cn k. Place the next 3 on a cn in front of the
work, knit k3, knit the 3 from the cn k, p2.

Repeat rows 1–7 until the edge reaches
around half of the heart, and cast (bind)
off. Knit two identical cable edges.

Assembly:
Sew in all the loose ends. Fold the wool fabric
in half with the backside facing up. Place the
heart on the fabric and sketch around. Cut
out with a 1cm (⅜in) seam allowance.
Place the heart and the two layers of fabric on top
of each other and sew together so that the right
side is out. Leave approximately 10cm (4in) on one
side. Stuff carded wool between the two fabric
layers or use a heart-shaped pillow. Stitch up.
Hide the edges with the knitted cable that you
sew onto the work with small stitches – first
on the front side and then on the back.

Funky flowers

Materials
Black fabric: 42 x 62cm (16½ x 24½in)
Light green wool fabric: 42 x 81cm
(16½ x 32in) for fold and front piece, and
42 x 62cm (16½ x 24½in) for the back.

Yarn
Here you can use different kinds and colours
of leftover yarn. To make the flowers look
exactly the same as in the pictures, use:
Babyull from Dale Garn (wool)
50g (1¾oz) orange no. 2908
50g (1¾oz) light pink no. 4504
50g (1¾oz) dark pink no. 4516

Falk from Dale Garn (wool)
50g (1¾oz) orange-red no. 3608
50g (1¾oz) purple no. 5036
50g (1¾oz) green no. 8817

2.5mm (size 2) crochet hooks

Finished size: 40 x 60cm (16 x 24in)

Wrap yarn in colour A (see next page)
approx 8 times to form a ring, this will
be the centre base of the flower.

Round 1: Start the row with 2 ch = 1 dc.
Crochet 28 sc ino the yarn ring.
Round 2: Crochet 1 dc in each sc, 28 dc in total.
Round 3: Switch to colour B. Crochet only in
the back loop of the sts. *2 dc in first st,
1 in the next*. Repeat from * to * until the end of
the row. Then you should have 45 sts in total.
Round 4: Crochet only in the back loop
of the sts. *1 dc in each st 3 times, 2 ch*.
Repeat from * to * until the end of the row.
Finish with 1 dc in each st 3 times.
Round 5: Switch to colour C. *Crochet
1 sc, 2 ch, 1 ch around the ch loop,
then 2 ch and skip 3 sts*. Repeat from
* to * until the end of the row.
Round 6: *Crochet 2 dc, 2 ch, 2 dc
around the ch loop, then 2 ch*. Repeat
from * to * until the end of the row.
Round 7: Switch to colour D. *Crochet 3 dc,
2 ch, 3 dc around the ch loop, then 2 ch*.
Repeat from * to * until the end of the row.
Round 8: *Crochet 4 dc, 2 ch, 4 dc
around the ch, then 2 ch*. Repeat from
* to * until the end of the row.

Leaves:
Use green yarn.
Round 1: Crochet 3 ch, 1 extra ch when you turn.
Round 2: 1 sc, 3 dc in next st, 1 sc,
1 extra ch when you turn.
Round 3: 2 sc, 3 dc in next st, 2 sc,
1 extra ch when you turn.
Rooud 4: 1 sc in second st, 1 sc, 3 dc in
next st, 2 sc, 1 extra ch when you turn.
Round 5: 2 sc, 1 dc, 3 dc in next st,
2 sc, 1 extra ch when you turn.
Round 6: 2 sc, 2 dc, 3 dc in next st, 2 dc, 2 sc

Embroidery and assembly:
Secure all loose ends and press (iron) the pieces.

Position the small flower in the centre of the black fabric and the two remaining flowers on each side. Pin the flowers in place and sew using small stitches in each tip. Sew the stems with green yarn using chain stitch. Position the leaves and sew.

Use a white coloured pencil and sketch out curved lines to come out of the flowers. It doesn't matter if they are not identical. Sew with pink yarn using outline stitch. Sew French knots around the middle flower and a small pink flower in each corner made from five loop stitches.

Turn the fabric. Use a white pencil and draw a line around the work, approximately 2–3cm (¾–1¼in) inside the edge. Cut out on the line using zigzag scissors.

Turn the work again; draw up a new line about 1.5cm (¾in) inside the zigzag edge. Place the fabric on the green front piece. Use green thread to sew outline stitches through both layers along the line.

Press (iron) the work carefully on the backside. Place the front and back pieces right sides together and sew the pillow with fold as described in Good Advice: here the fold is on the right hand side.

	Flower 1	Flower 2	Flower 3
Colour A	orange-red	orange-red	orange
Colour B	orange	pink	purple
Colour C	purple	orange-red	orange
Colour D	orange-red		pink

Granny pillow

Materials
7 buttons

Yarn
Mandarin petit from Sandnesgarn (cotton)
100g (3½oz) white no. 101
100g (3½oz) red no. 4418
50g (1¾oz) pink no. 4505
50g (1¾oz) dark pink no. 4517

3mm (size 3) crochet hooks

Finished size: 40 x 40cm (16 x 16in)

Front piece:
Crochet 16 granny squares in total:
Crochet 4 ch with pink yarn and make a ring with 1 sl st. Crochet 2 ch that is first dc, and continue with 7 dc so that you have 8 in total. Finish the row with 1 sl st. Switch to dark pink yarn and crochet 2 sl st between every dc in the first row so that you get 16 dc in total. Finish the row with 1 sl st. Switch to red yarn and crochet 2 dc between every dc in the last row so that you get 32 dc. Finish the row with 1 sl st. Continue with red yarn on the next row, but crochet every other 1 dc and 2 dc between every dc in the previous row. When you are at the end of the row you should have 48 dc in total. Finish with 1 sl st. Switch to white yarn and *crochet 3 dc in the same gap, 1 ch, skip 3 red dc and crochet 3 new dc in the next gap, 2 ch, skip 3 red dc and crochet 3 new dc in the next gap. Then crochet 3 ch and 3 new dc in the same gap. Continue with 1 ch, skip 3 red dc and crochet 3 new dc in the next gap, 1 ch*. Repeat from * to * until the end of the row. Finish with 1 sl st.
Last row: Continue the same way with 3 dc in each gap and 1 ch between while you increase in the corners. See description of granny squares in Good Advice.

Secure all loose ends and crochet together as shown in Good Advice.

Back piece, bottom part:
Crochet 76 ch with red yarn, turn *crochet 1 ch and 76 sc *. Repeat from * to * until you have 4 rows of red. Switch to pink yarn and crochet 4 rows of sc in the same way. Repeat the stripes of red and pink until you have 9 red and 9 pink stripes. Switch to red yarn and crochet 6 rows of sc.

Back piece, top part:
Crochet 76 ch with red yarn, turn and crochet
1 ch and 76 sc. On row 3, crochet buttonhole
like this: 1 ch, 8 sc, *2 ch, skip 2 sc and
continue with 8 sc*. Repeat from * to * 6 times,
crochet 2 ch, skip 2 sc and finish with 7 sc.
Next row: 1 ch when you turn, 7 sc, *2 sc around
the ch loop, 8 sc*. Repeat from * to * 6 times,
and finish with 2 sc around the ch loop, 7 sc.
Switch to pink yarn and continue with the stripes
until you have 4 red and 3 pink stripes in total.

Assembly:
Secure all loose ends. Sew together the two
back pieces on the sides. The top piece should
lie above the bottom piece so that the two red
stripes overlap. Sew on buttons that fit the holes.
Place the front and back pieces wrong sides
together and crochet the two layers together from
the front side with sc and white yarn. Finish off
with a round of picot: 1 sc, *3 ch, skip 1 sc and
crochet 1 sc*. Repeat from * to * the whole way
around the pillow. Don't skip 1 sc in the corners.

Granny blanket

Yarn
Mandarin Petit from Sandnesgarn (cotton)
300g (10½oz) white no. 101
50g (1¾oz) red no. 4418
50g (1¾oz) pink no. 4505
50g (1¾oz) dark pink no. 4517
50g (1¾oz) old rose 4007
50g (1¾oz) spring green 8514
50g (1¾oz) yellow-green no. 8722
PT Pandora from rauma ullvarefabrikk (cotton)
50g (1¾oz) red no. 259
50g (1¾oz) pink no. 251
100g (3½oz) old rose

150g (5oz) spring green no. 280

ECO Baby cotton from Marks & Kattens (mercerized cotton)
50g (1¾oz) light miss no. 906

The blanket weighs 600g (1lb 5oz) in total. Here I have chosen as many shades as possible, but it is not necessary to buy all the different yarns from the different brands.

3mm (size 3) crochet hooks

You need 140 granny squares in total

Finished size: 1.1 x 1.55m (1¼ x 1¾yds)

Square type 1:
Crochet granny square (see Good Advice).
A: Red, light green, old rose: 20 squares.
B: Red, dark pink, spring green: 22 squares.
C: Red, pink, spring green: 16 squares.
D: Red, pink, yellow-green: 12 squares.
E: Red, red, red: 12 squares.
F: Red, pink, moss green: 2 squares.
G: Red, dark pink, yellow-green: 7 squares.
H: Red, old rose, spring green: 28 squares.
I: Red, dark pink, moss green: 2 squares.

Square type 2:
Crochet 4 ch with pink yarn and make a ring with 1 sl st. Crochet 2 ch as the first dc, and continue with 7 dc so you have 8 dc in total. Finish the row with 1 sl st.
Switch to dark pink yarn and crochet 2 dc between every dc in the first row so you get 16 dc in total. Finish the row with 1 sl st.
Switch to red yarn and crochet 2 dc between every dc in the previous row so that you get 32 dc in total. Finish the row with 1 sl st.
Continue the next row with red yarn, crochet every other 1 dc and 2 dc between every dc in the previous row. When you have finished with the entire round you should have 48 dc in total. Finish with 1 sl st.
Switch to white yarn and *crochet 3 dc in the same gap, 1 ch, skip 3 red dc and crochet 3 new dc in the next gap, 1 ch, skip 3 red dc and crochet 3 new dc in the next gap. Crochet 3 ch, then 3 new dc in the same gap. Continue with 1 ch, skip 3 red dc and crochet 3 new dc in the next gap, 1 ch*. Repeat from * to * until the end of the row. Finish with 1 sl st.
Last row: Continue the same way with 3 dc in each gap and 1 ch in-between while you increase in the corners. See instructions about Granny Squares in Good Advice.

2: Pink, dark pink, red 17 patches.

Assembly:
Secure all the loose ends. Crochet the squares together, one row at the time merged together (see Good Advice).

The diagram opposite shows how the patches are positioned within the blanket:

E	B	B	A	2	A	H	H	C	E
B	C	H	B	D	2	A	H	2	H
C	2	H	D	B	F	H	B	D	2
A	H	2	H	E	B	G	D	C	B
E	A	H	A	D	H	2	H	H	E
H	H	B	A	H	A	H	2	E	H
C	2	A	C	B	2	C	G	C	H
A	B	E	H	G	H	E	B	C	G
H	G	H	2	H	D	B	I	A	E
E	A	B	H	2	F	A	A	B	H
B	H	A	A	D	B	C	C	G	B
2	B	D	C	C	F	G	F	2	D
E	D	2	B	H	A	I	D	C	2
A	B	C	2	D	B	C	A	A	E

Silk pillow with knitted edge

Materials
Red silk: 45 x 45cm (18 x 18in) for the
front piece, 35 x 45cm (14 x 18in) and
13 x 45cm (5¼ x 18in) for the back piece
Zip 35cm (14in)

Yarn
Spun silk with beads and sequins from
Artyarns (silk)
50g (1¾oz) hibiscus

3mm (size 3) needles

Finished size: 43 x 43cm (17 x 17in)
Pillow 40 x 40cm (16 x 16in)

Assembly:
Overstitch around the fabric pieces. Sew the
zip on to the back piece (see Good Advice).
Place the front and back pieces right
sides together and sew around.
Cut off excess fabric at the corners, press
the seams apart and reverse the work.

Pin along the edge of the pillow and sew
a 1.5cm (½in) seam inside the edge.

Sew the knitting together using kitchener stitches
to make a ring. Measure the ribbon to make four
identical parts. Place one part on each side of the
pillow, approximately 0.5–1cm (¼–½in) inside the
edge. Make sure you have enough ribbon for the
corners. Pin and sew by hand along the inside.
Avoid sewing through both layers of fabric.

Sometimes we end up with lovely leftover yarn that we don't know how to use. Other times we find exclusive, expensive yarn that we are tempted to buy but can't afford too much of. What do we do with the yarn when we don't have enough for a garment or pillow?

Here I chose to knit a ribbon and sew it to a simple silk pillow. The length of the ribbon determined how big the pillow could be.

BLACK AND WHITE

EBONY AND IVORY

"Ebony and ivory" wrote Paul McCartney, and sang a duet with Stevie Wonder about black and white keys side by side on the piano "...in perfect harmony."

Sheep white and sheep black were the yarn colours they had the easiest access to back in the day. Other colours required considerably more work.

The first selbu garments in black and white were supposed to have been delivered to Husfliden in Trondheim for resale in 1897. The monochrome mittens quickly gained popularity. They became a permanent accessory to sports outfits, especially ski equipment, but you could also see them on the main street of Oslo, Karl Johan. Abroad they also wanted Norwegian knitwear. Hand-knitted mittens and gloves with selbu pattern are among the best sellers at craftwork outlets around the country.

Knitting contributed to a valuable income in Selbu during the interwar period. Men and young boys knitted and it was common to knit while you were walking along the roads. If you were good, you could knit a pair of mittens in a day. The best make two pairs. The high demand led to poor quality of the products. The knitters switched to coarser yarn and thicker needles to comply with the volume of orders. The merchants therefore demanded better quality and a standardization of the gloves and mittens. Labelling and inspections of the products were introduced in 1934, and still the knitwear from Selbu is labelled with a special seal.

The first man

Materials
Fabric for back piece: natural coloured wool,
66 x 52cm (26 x 20½in)

Yarn
Tweed from Rowan (wool)
100g (3½oz) light grey no. 5668 d
100g (3½oz) dark grey/black no. 6035

3.5mm (size 4) needles

Finished size: 50 x 50cm (20 x 20in)

Crochet 114 ch with light grey and make a ring
with 1 sl st. Crochet sc, first 4 rows of light
grey, then follow the pattern which goes over
100 sts. See description in Good Advice on how
to crochet sc with multiple colours. Read the
pattern (from Patterns section) from right to left,
bottom to top, just like when you knit. The extra
14 sts are always crocheted with light grey.

The work will stretch and become crinkled
while you crochet but this will disappear
when you block the work towards the end.

All the threads follow the work all the way around.
The threads that don't form a sc lie hidden
inside the sts. Make sure you don't tighten these
threads; this will make the work uneven.

It can be a good idea to colour the rows that
you have finished while you work your way
up the diagram. This will make it easier to
know where you are at any point of time.

Continue until you have finished the diagram.

Assembly:
Sew in all loose ends and sew a tight zigzag
on each side of the central stitch in the
light grey areas. Cut the work apart.
Block the work (see Good Advice).

Sew pillow with fold and described in Good Advice.

Titanic

Materials
Fabric for back piece: natural coloured wool,
57 x 62cm (22½ x 24½in)

Yarn
Sterk from Du Store Alpakka
(alpaca/merino wool/nylon)
150g (5oz) sheep white no. 806
100g (3½in) black/dark grey no. 808

3.5mm (size 4) crochet hooks

Finished size: 42 x 60cm (16½ x 24in)

Crochet 132 ch in white yarn, and make a ring with 1 sl st. Continue with sc, first 4 rows of white, then follow the diagram (see Patterns section) that goes over 120 sts. See instructions on how you crochet sc with multiple colours in Good Advice. The diagram is read from right to left, bottom to top, just like when you knit. Always crochet the extra 12 sts in white.

The work will stretch and become crinkled while you crochet but this will disappear when you block the work towards the end.

All the threads follow the work all the way around. The threads that don't form a sc lie hidden inside the st. Make sure you don't tighten these threads; this will make the work uneven.

It can be a good idea to colour the rows that you have finished while you work your way up the diagram. This will make it easier to know where you are at any point of time.

Continue until you have finished the diagram.

Assembly:
Sew in all loose ends and sew a tight zigzag on each side of the central stitch in the white areas. Cut the work apart. Block the work as shown in Good Advice.

Sew the pillow with fold (see Good Advice).

Norwegian news

Yarn
Tweed from Rowan (wool)
100g (3½oz) light grey no. 5668 D
100g (3½oz) dark grey/black no. 6035
Natural coloured wool: 58 x 64cm (23 x 25¼in)

3.5mm (size 4) needles

Finished size: 42 x 62cm (16½ x 24½in)

Crochet 134 ch in light grey yarn and make a ring with 1 sl st. Continue with sc, first 3 rows of white, then follow the diagram (see Patterns section) that goes over 120 sts. See Good Advice for how to crochet sc with multiple colours. The diagram is read from right to left, bottom to top, just like when you knit. Always crochet the extra 14 sts in light grey.

The work will stretch towards the left and become crinkled while you crochet but this will disappear when you block the work towards the end.

All the threads follow the work all the way around. The threads that don't form a sc lie hidden inside the st. Make sure you don't tighten these threads; this will make the work uneven.

It is good idea to colour the rows that you have finished while you work your way up the diagram. This will make it easier to know where you are at any point of time.

Continue until you have finished the diagram.

Assembly:
Sew in all loose ends and sew a tight zigzag on each side of the central stitch in the light grey areas. Cut the work apart.

Block the work as shown in Good Advice.

Sew the pillow with fold (see Good Advice).

Marilyn

Finished size: 50 x 50cm (20 x 20in)

Overstitch around the linen fabric before you start sewing. Find the centre of the fabric and place the subject about 1cm (⅜in) above. Follow the diagram in the Patterns section.

Assembly:
Sew in the zip on the back piece as described in Good Advice. Place the front and back pieces right sides together and sew around. Press (iron) the seams apart, cut off excess fabric at the corners and reverse the work.

All you knit is love

Materials
Zip 40cm (16in)

Yarn
Sterk from Du Store Alpakka
(alpaca/merino wool/nylon)
200g (7oz) sheep white no. 806
100g (3½oz) black/dark grey no. 808

3.5mm (size 4) needles

Finished size: 50 x 50cm (20 x 20in)

CO 236 sts in sheep white yarn on a circular needle and knit k. Knit 5 rows before you start the diagram in the Patterns section that goes over 118 sts. Knit the same on both sides or skip the heart on the backside. (It should be 5 white sts on each side of the "paper".)

It is a good idea to colour the rows that you have finished while you work your way up the diagram. This will make it easier to know where you are at any point of time. It is not necessary to copy every single "word" to get the same look. You can always choose the length of the words yourself.

You will have pretty long leaps of yarn in some places in this work. It is therefore important to weave the yarn along on the wrong side. Make sure you don't tighten the thread too much.

Continue until you have finished the diagram and finish with 5 rows of white before you cast (bind) off.

Assembly:
Sew in all loose ends and press (iron) the work carefully. Sew in the zip as described in Good Advice. Sew together the top and the sides with backstitches on the right side. The seam is a part of the appearance and makes the cushion look more like a newspaper.

Zebra and leopard

Yarn
Sterk from Du Store Alpakka
(alpaca/merino wool/nylon)
100g (3½oz) sheep white no. 806
100g (3½oz) black no. 809

3.5mm (size 4) needles

Finished size: 30 x 50cm (12 x 20in)

CO 224 sts on a circular needle with white yarn. Knit 110 sts k from the diagram in the Patterns section, p2 with white yarn, using a stitch holder in the side. Knit 110 sts k from the diagram and p2 in white yarn. Use a stitch holder on this side also. Continue this way until the work is complete. Cast (bind) off with black yarn.

It is a good idea to copy the diagram and mark off when you finish a row, using a coloured pencil for example. In this way you will always know where you are at any point in time.

Assembly:
Press (iron) the work carefully. Sew together the top and about 8cm (3¼in) on each side at the bottom with kitchener stitches. Sew a white ribbon on the inside of the remaining sts and sew buttons in place (see Good Advice).

Music to your ears

Overstitch around the linen fabric before you start. Find the centre and follow the diagram in the Patterns section. The red square marks the middle of the pillow and is not to be sewn.

Materials
White linen, 10 threads per cm,
52 x 52cm (20½ x 20½in)
Back piece: 43 x 52cm (17 x 20½in) and
13 x 52cm (5¼ x 20½in)

Zip 40cm (16in)

Yarn
DMC mouliné fine yarn:
6 skeins black no. 310
Sew with split yarn (3 threads) over
2 x 2 threads

Assembly:
Sew in the zip on the back piece (see Good Advice). Place the front and back pieces right sides together and sew around. Press the seams apart, cut off excess fabric at the corners and reverse the work.

White wonder

Materials
White linen: 140 x 57cm (55 x 22½in)

Yarn
PT Petunia from Rauma Ullvarefabrikk
(cotton)
350g (12oz) white no. 221

4mm (size 6) needles

Finished size: 55 x 55cm (22 x 22in)
(pillow 50 x 50cm (20 x 20in))

CO 118 sts and knit back and forth.
Row 1 (the right side of the pillow):
K1, p1, repeat from * to *
until the end of the row.
Row 2: *K1, p1*, repeat from * to *
until the end of the row.
Row 3: *P1, k1*, repeat from * to *
until the end of the row.
Row 4: *P1, k1*, repeat from * to *
until the end of the row.
Rows 5–8: Repeat rows 1–4.
Rows 9–10: Repeat rows 1–2.
Row 11: *K1, p1*, repeat from * to *
6 times, **p2, yo1, k2, tk2tog, k3,
p1, k3, k2tog, k2, yo1, p2, place the next st
on a cn behind the work, knit next st k, then
knit the st on the cn k, p2, place the next st
on a cn behind the work, knit the next st k,
then knit the st on the cn k**. Repeat from
** to ** 3 times, then p2, yo1, k2, tk2tog,
k3, p1, k3, k2tog, k2, yo1, p2. Finally
k1, p1, repeat from * to * 6 times.
Row 12: *K1, p1*, repeat from * to *
6 times, k2, p7, k1, p7, k2, **p2, k2,
p2, k2, p7, k1, p7, k2**. Repeat from
** to ** 3 times. Finally *k1, p1*,
repeat from * to * 6 times.
Row 13: *P1, k1*, repeat from * to *
6 times, **p2, k1, yo1, k2, tk2tog, k2,
p1, k2, k2tog, k2, yo1, k1, p2,
place the next st on a cn behind the work,
knit next st k, then knit the st on the cn k, p2,
place the next st on a cn behind the work,
knit the next st k, then knit the st on the cn
k**. Repeat from ** to ** 3 times, then p2,
k1, yo1, k2, tk2tog, k2, p1, k2,
k2tog, k2, yo1, k1, p2. Finally *p1,
k1*, repeat from * to * 6 times.
Row 14: *P1, k1*, repeat from * to *
6 times, k2, p7, k1, p7, k2, **p2, k2,
p2, k2, p7, k1, p7, k2**, repeat from
to * 3 times. Finally, *p1, k1 *,
repeat from * to * 6 times.
Row 15: *K1, p1*, repeat from * to *
6 times, **p2, k2, yo1, k2, tk2tog, k1,
p1, k1, k2tog, k2, yo1, k2, p2,
place the next st on a cn behind the work,
knit next st k, then knit the st on the cn k,
p2, place the next st on a cn behind the work,
knit the next st k, then knit the st on the cn
k**. Repeat from ** to ** 3 times, then p2,
k1, yo1, k2, tk2tog, k1, p1, k1,
k2tog, k2, yo1, k2, p2. Finally *k1, p1*,
repeat from * to * 6 times.

Row 16: Repeat row 12.
Row 17: *P1, k1*, repeat from * to * 6 times,
**p2, k3, yo1, k2, tk2tog, p1, k2tog, k2, yo1, k3, p2,
place the next st on a cn behind the work,
knit next st k, then knit the st on the cn k, p2,
place the next st on a cn behind the work, knit
the next st k, then knit the st on the cn k**.
Repeat from ** to ** 3 times, then p2, k3,
yo1, k2, tk2tog, p1, k2tog, k2, yo1, k3, p2.
Finally *p1, k1*, repeat from * to * 6 times.
Row 18: Repeat row 14.

Repeat rows 11–18 until the work
measures approximately 50cm (20in).

Repeat row 1–10 and cast (bind) off.

Assembly:
Sew in all loose ends.

Take advantage of the selvage of the linen fabric if
possible. Place the front piece on the linen fabric,
5.5cm (2¼in) from the edge, and pin. Sew together
with a small overstitch towards the fold. Tack
(baste) the remaining sides. Sew the pillow with fold
(see Good Advice). The fold is here 30cm (12in). This
can be adjusted with the fold of the linen fabric.
Cut off excess fabric in the corners, and press (iron)
the seams apart before you reverse the work.
Tack (baste) about 2.5cm (1in) inside the edge of
the moss stitched edge the whole way around so
that you can fit a 50 x 50cm (20 x 20in) pillow.

GOOD ADVICE

FROM A STITCH PERSPECTIVE

When I was a young student almost 30 years ago, I had the idea of having my own weaving workshop. I rented an old servant's room and spent hours and hours weaving. I made everything from soft woollen scarves to large tapestries. The products were mostly traded among friends and acquaintances, but I also attended an occasional trade fair.

It is long since I ended my time as a weaver. But I have always enjoyed making things, whether it's with yarn or fabric. Some items have been useful and practical, while other stuff has been mostly for decoration. I have experimented with knitting, crochet, patchwork and embroidery – among other crafts – and have made for friends, family and for myself. And although there are some half-finished works in a drawer here and a locker there, most of my projects are complete. The joy is just as significant during the making of the project as it is after its completion.

In the past, less scholarly students could be the kings of P.E. or of woodwork class. Today it is difficult to excel in arts and crafts, even if one is both creative and dexterous one still needs to have an overview of important artists and designers. And in P.E. one must do well on theoretical tests of physics of the body and biology to achieve the As and Bs. If you have trouble studying, one can have difficulty and the grades can turn out to be mediocre.

Some theory can be good but it is too highly emphasized in today's schools. One cannot learn how to swim by reading a book. If you want to learn how to ride a bike, you have to practice. There is actually a great amount of knowledge that can't be transferred through theory. We have, for example, a great boat-building tradition in Norway. For more than 1000 years we have built world-class sea vessels. The craftsmen know what makes one subject better than others, even if it's hard to explain. It may be the way the tree grew, the direction of the fibres, the weight of the wood, or a combination of many things. This is learned knowledge and cannot be taught through books. It is acquired through experience.

Many might say I am reactionary to think that embroidery and knitting are valuable subjects. But needlework techniques strengthen coping skills and the well-being of both children and adolescents, and creativity is a prerequisite for change and progress. Also fine motor skills are learned when striving with needle and thread or sticky knitting needles. Fine motor skills are essential if we want skilled dentists and surgeons in the future. With our desire for a perfect look, it is even more important that the doctors master both tailoring, embroidery and fine darning.

Single crochet with multiple colours:

Tapestry crochet is among others known to originate from Guatemala, Cameroon, Turkey and Finland. Norway has a tradition of making crochet rose tapestry gloves in Flesberg in Numedal, and patterned works have also been found in Morgedal and Setesdal. In the last few years we've also seen this technique used for making hats. It is not that commonly used even though it gives great possibilities to create patterns that are difficult to make without the large yarn leaps of other techniques.

To obtain a smooth and uniform appearance, you should not crochet back and forth. Instead, you should crochet in a circle. To make a pillow, you can create it from one large crochet piece and either fold it in half or crochet a few extra stitches then cut the work apart at the end. The edges are then sewn with a machine before cutting. Alternatively you can start in the centre of the circle and work your way out, ring by ring.

1. Begin with chain stitches and turn these into a circle with a slip stitch.

2. Single crochet around both loops and thread(s) that are not a part of the pattern. It is also possible to crochet only around the back loop – as was done traditionally in Flesberg – but then the work will have horizontal stripes.

3. The colour is easily switched by changing position of the threads; the one that was lying passively inside the stitch is now active, and vice versa.

4. The last single crochet before the colour change will lie over the new stitch so it will appear like you did something wrong. This will even out in the next row.

5. If you want a cleaner appearance, you can switch colours in the middle of a stitch. Then you stick the needle through the stitch loop, pull the yarn through and pick up the new colour to complete the stitch. This method is not traditional in Norway and is not used in this book.

6. The work will stretch and become crinkled when you crochet but this will disappear when you block the work after you are finished.

7. All the yarn follows the stitches all the way around and the threads that are not used in a single crochet remain hidden inside the stitches. Make sure you don't tighten these threads; this will make the work uneven. Large works can be a challenge and it can be wise to measure the width along the way.

8. If you are crocheting from a diagram, read it from right to left and bottom to top, in the same way as in knitting diagrams. It might be a good idea to colour the rows you have completed as you work your way up the pattern. This will make it easier to know where you are at all times. On www.youtube.com you can find several videos of how to single crochet with multiple colours.

Blocking your work:

Many works stretch in one direction or another while you make them. Others contract so you can have difficulties seeing the pattern. Ironing, pressing and steaming rarely helps; you simply have to block out the work.

You will need stainless steel pins and a porous board, e.g. polystyrene, styrofoam or cork. I've invested in two 40 x 60cm (16 x 24in) corkboards from Ikea. If I can't fit the work on one, I can simply put them together. I've kept the plastic on, but alternatively you can place a clean piece of paper on top of the boards when needed so you don't get colour from wet cork and other materials on your fabrics.

It can be of great help to draw some orthogonal help lines onto the board or paper.

Place the work onto the board and start to attach one long side with a few pins. Stretch and pull the work until it forms your desired shape. Pin onto the opposite side and do the same on the two remaining sides. Use a tape measure and square ruler while working. Don't stop until you are satisfied with the shape. Gradually add the pins closer and closer together. You should have about 1 pin per cm when the work is blocked.

Spray the work with lukewarm, clean water until it is completely wet. If you don't have a spray bottle, you can clean out an old window washing spray bottle, or similar. The work should stay blocked while it dries for at least one day. Don't remove the pins until you are absolutely sure that the work is dry.

Making neat corners:

When you sew together two pieces with right sides together, it can be challenging to make the corners look attractive. They can easily turn out rounded or blunt when the work is reversed. The reason is that the corner is too cramped. To obtain neat corners it is important to cut off excess fabric. Therefore cut the fabric about 2mm (1⁄16in) from the seam. When the work is reversed, use a blunt needle and carefully pull out the corners. Alternatively, push from the inside. It is important not to be too eager; if you pull too hard you can easily pull out the whole seam (remember that almost the entire seam allowance is cut off).

Sewing pillows with folds:

This example measures 50 x 50cm (20 x 20in) finished.

Cut out one piece of fabric measuring 52 x 52cm (20½ x 20½in), and one that measures 66 x 52cm (26 x 20½in) and overstitch around the fabrics. You will then have approximately 15cm (6in) for the fold on the front piece. If you don't have enough fabric you should have enough for 10cm (4in).

Place the two fabrics right sides together, pin and sew together about 10cm (4in) up each side with 1cm (⅜in) seam allowance on the front piece and 15cm (6in) seam allowance on the back. Fold one of the pieces backwards by 15cm (6in) so that you have two equal squares. Pin the two layers and sew along the three remaining sides. Cut off the corners and iron the seams apart before you reverse the work.

The edges on the front piece are sewn with small stitches.

If you think the fold stands out too much, you can simply attach small buttons with simple loops, or tied ribbon.

How to sew in a zip by hand:

Place the bottom of the front and back pieces against each other with the right side up, and sew carefully together using a help thread in a contrasting colour. Place the zip underneath the joint. Make sure it lies in the middle and secure with a couple pins at each end.

Turn the work and secure the lock with pins. Make sure it lies exactly above the joint. Tack (baste) if you find it necessary.

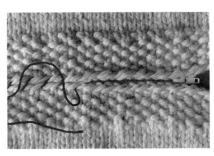

Turn the work back and sew in the zip with small backstitches from the right side. Use double sewing thread or if the yarn you've knitted with is not too thick, you might also be able to use this. Follow the stitch rows.

When the zip is well attached, remove the help thread. Now you can sew together the sides and the top.

How to sew a zip with a sewing machine:

Overstitch around all loose edges. Place the front and back pieces right sides together, find the middle and mark where you want the zip. Sew each side up to the zip, preferably with a 2cm (¾in) seam allowance.

Reverse the work and place the zip in the split. Secure with pins and sew. Start on the left side just below the lock, continue down to the bottom of the zip, sew right across, and continue on the opposite side. When approaching the lock, leave the needle in the work, lift the foot and help the lock past. Continue to sew all the way up, sew right across and back down to where you started. Use a zip foot.

Place the fabric on the ironing board and press (iron) the seams apart. Press firmly as if the seam was of the entire width.

It is often advisable to place the zip on the back of the pillow, e.g. 10cm (4in) from the top. Then you won't have a problem with any edges or lace around the work. Cut out two pieces of fabric for the backside. Add 1cm (⅜in) seam allowance on each end, and 2cm (¾in) for the zip seam, for example 33 x 52cm (13 x 20½in) and 13 x 52cm (4¼ x 20½in) for a pillow that measures 40 x 50cm (16 x 24in).

Place the two pieces right sides together and mark where you want to position the zip. Sew each side up to the zip, preferably with 2cm (¾in) seam allowance.

Press (iron) the seams apart. Press firmly as if there were stitching across the full width.

Reverse the work and place the zip in the split. Secure with pins and sew using a machine foot.

Now you can place the front and back pieces right sides together and sew around all four sides. Press the seams apart and cut off excess fabric at the corners. Open the zip and reverse the work. If you find it difficult to get the zip smooth and even, you can always

hide it underneath a fold. Then you have to add an additional 4cm (1½in) to the front piece. The example above would then have the pieces 33 x 52cm (13 x 20½in) and 17 x 52cm (6½ x 20½in).

Sew the zip as described. Fold the back piece in half so the fabric has wrong sides together with the fold 2cm (¾in) from the top part of the zip. Sew a seam right across the top part of the zip. Fold the fabric back and press (iron) the flap so that it covers the zip.

When sewing together the two pieces, make sure the flap lies in right direction.

Making closures with buttons
You can find elastic specially made with buttonholes. Place the elastic underneath the opening of the pillow and sew with small backstitches from the right side. Use double sewing thread and follow the rows. Sew buttons on the opposite side. You can also make loops yourself.

Secure the thread and make a loop that fits the button you want to use. Make sure the thread is secure in the other end. Alternatively, sew back so that the loop is double. Then sew buttonhole stitches tightly along the arch. Attach the thread before you make any other loops in the same manner.

Crocheting granny squares:
Granny squares can be made in countless ways. There are hundreds of different patterns, and this is one of the most common.

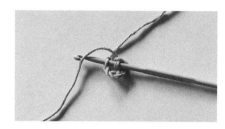

Start with 6 ch and make a ring with 1 sl st in the first ch.

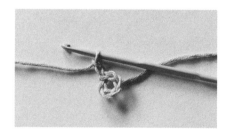

Make the first dc from 2 ch.

Do a cn and stick the needle through the ring. Pull the thread so you have 3 sts on the needle.

Finish dc by crocheting through the bottom 2 sts, then the top 2 sts.

Make 1 more dc in the same way. You now have a group of 3 dc. Then make 2 ch.

Continue with 3 new dc through the ch ring.

Then 3 new ch, 3 dc, 3 ch, 3 dc, and 3 ch.

Finish with 1 sl st at the top in the first dc. Cut the thread and pull through. You are now done with the first round.

Now you're ready for round two. Start by securing the new thread: stick the needle through the ch loop and pull through. Then pull both threads through st to form a loop. Continue with only one thread. Crochet the first dc from 2 ch, then 1 normal dc. Crochet 1 ch before continuing with 3 dc, 2 ch and 3 new dc in the corner.

Finish with 3 ch in the corner and 1 dc (so that you have 3 in total in the last group) before you cut the thread and pull it through the top of the first dc in this round.

Continue the same way. 1 ch, then 3 dc, 3 ch and 3 dc. Repeat for the whole round.

Continue this way every round. You decide if you want 2, 3 ,4 or 5 rounds.

All the threads have to be secured well. Use a darning needle and sew back and forth through the ch. This will make the threads invisible. Some choose to steam the patches or block them before putting them together. Other choose to finish the whole work before starting the afterwork.

Sewing buttonhole stitches:

Thread the needle so that you get a loop in the end you begin to sew. Stick the needle down next to the hole and up through the hole and loop. In this way you secure the thread while sewing the first stitch. When you have sewn buttonhole stitches the whole way around, secure the thread by sewing underneath the stitches on the backside for one and a half rounds while you tighten the thread so that all the buttonholes are about the same size.

Joining granny squares together:

Place the patches right sides together. Crochet 2 sc loosely in every "hole", and 1 ch between so you're able to reach the next hole without tightening the thread.

Crochet the patches together in rows then crochet the rows together. When you fold the patches back out the crochet will be like an invisible seam.

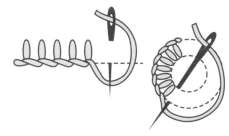

PATTERNS

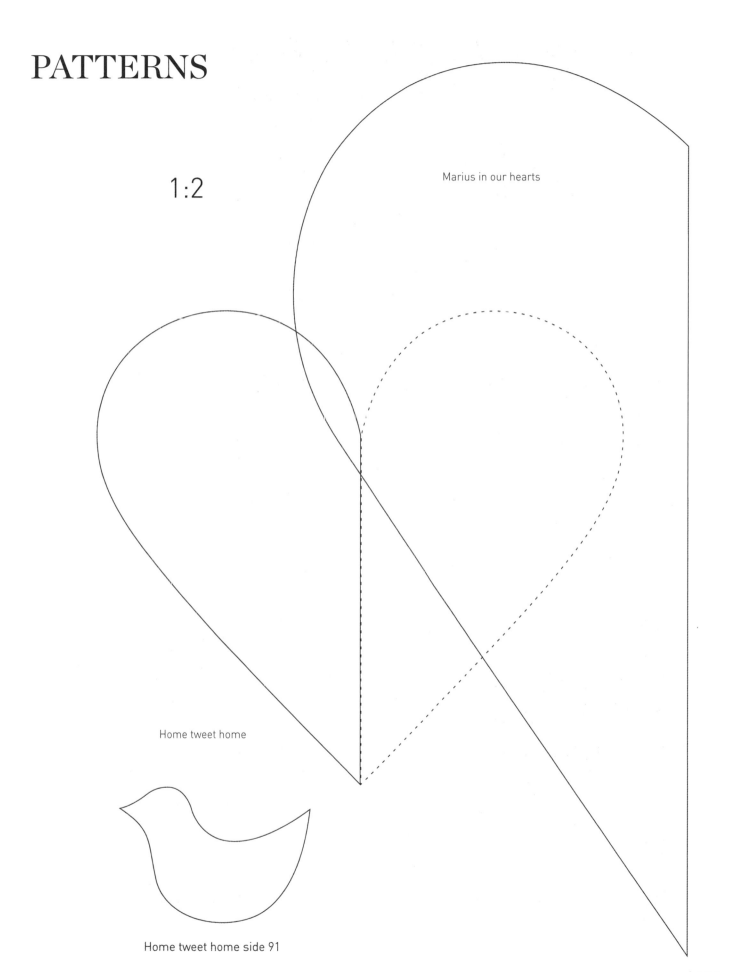

1:2

Marius in our hearts

Home tweet home

Home tweet home side 91

Pretty in pink

Pink borders

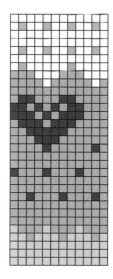

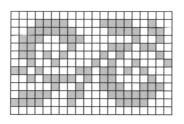

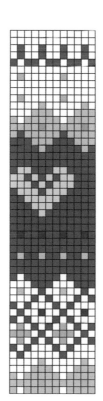

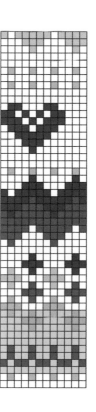

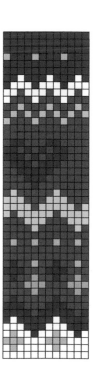

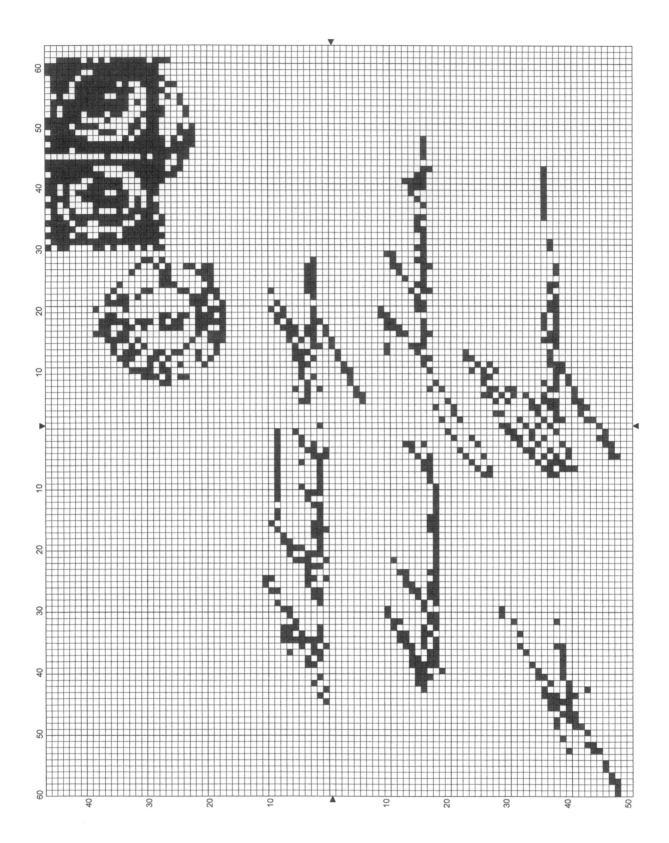

The love letter

The first man

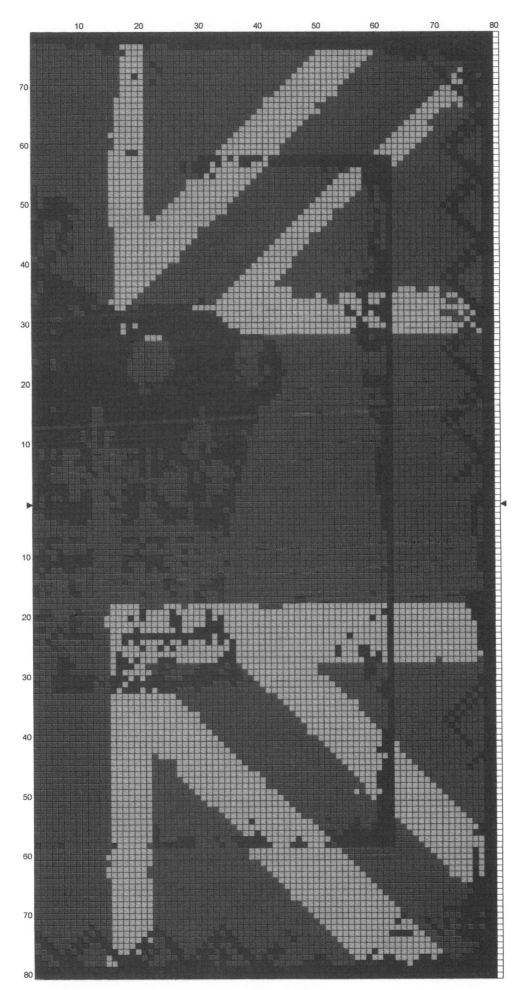

Titanic

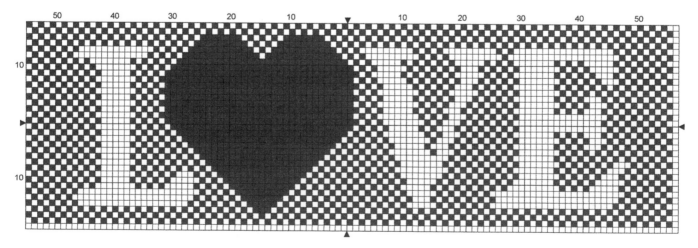

Love is...

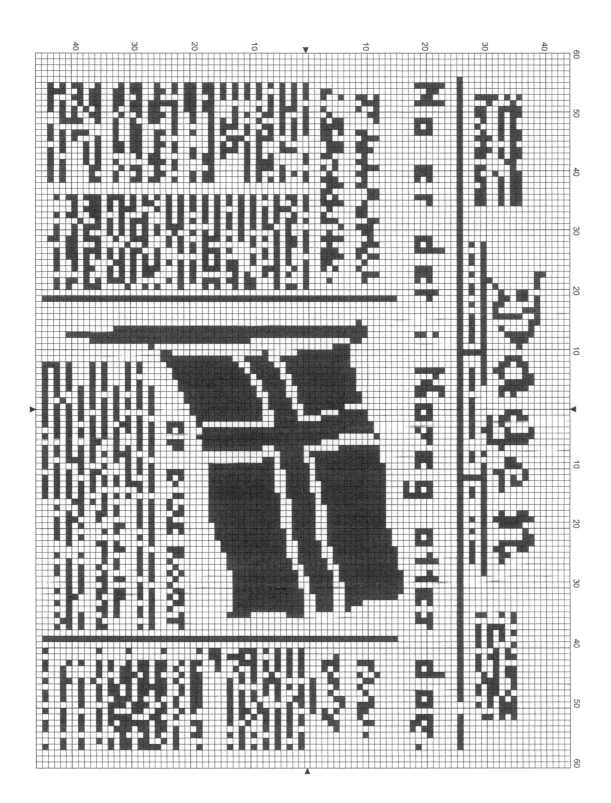

Norwegian news

Marilyn

All you knit is love

Music to
your ears

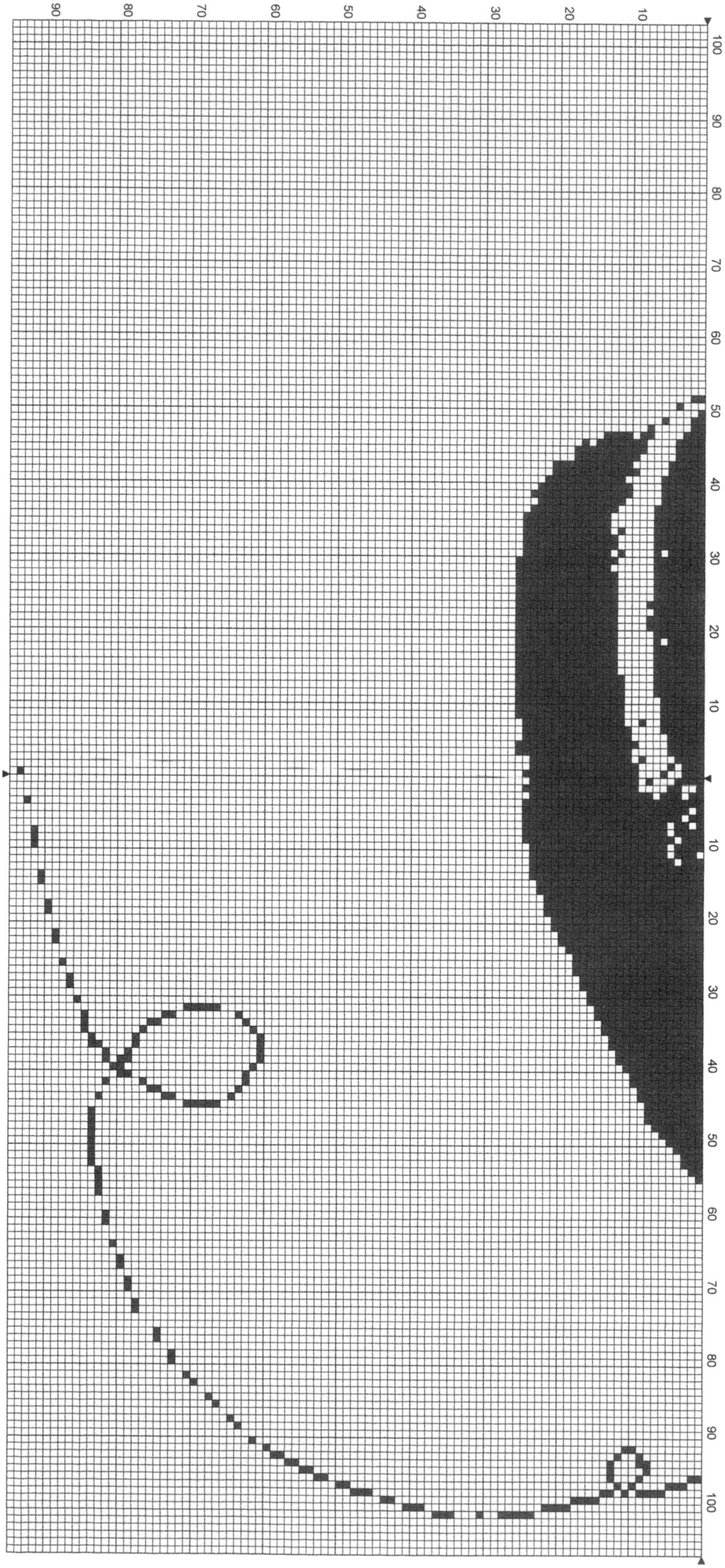

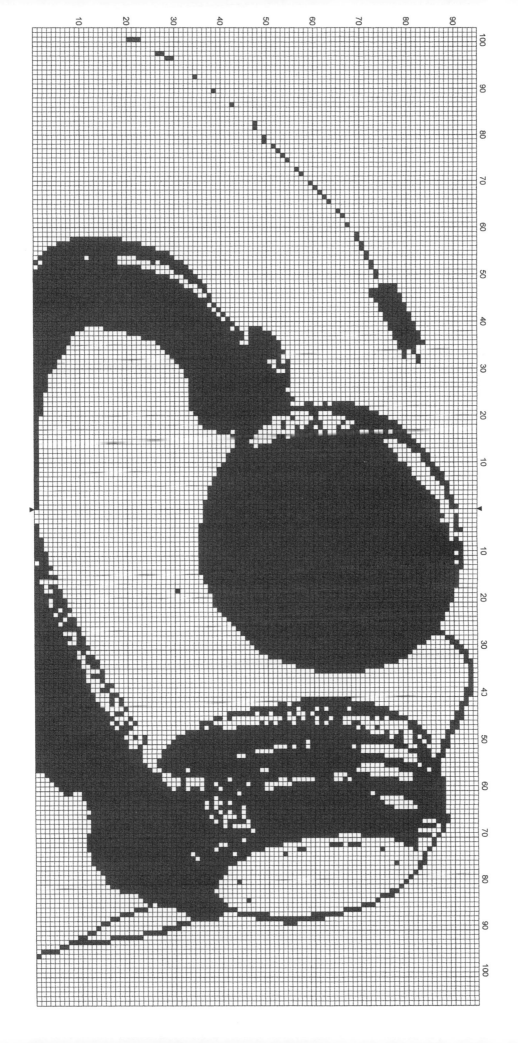

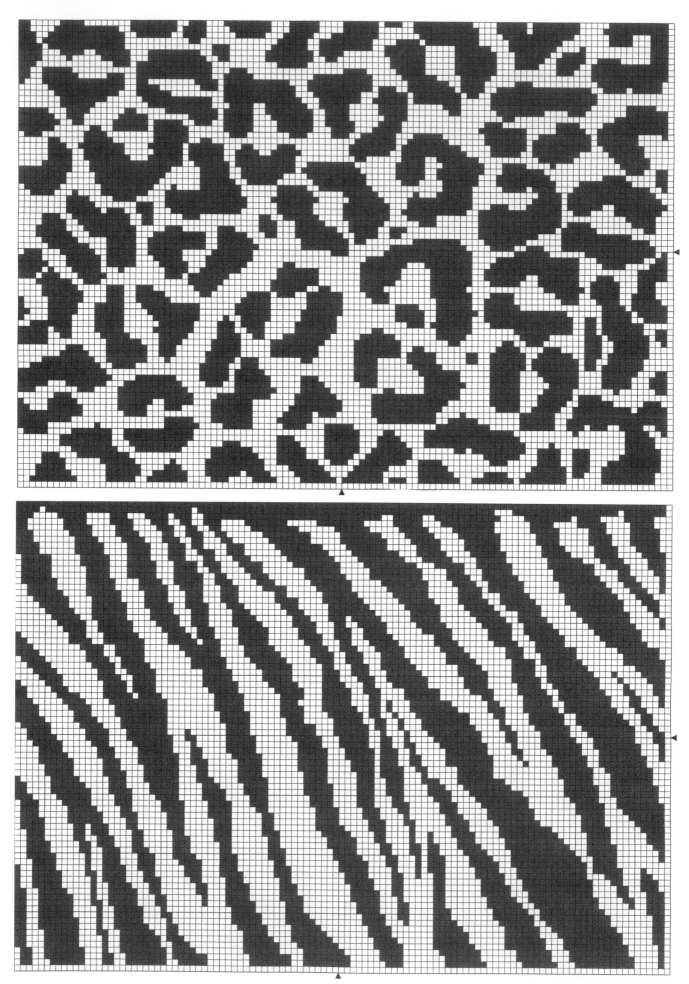

Zebra and leopard

SUPPLIERS

Artyarns
Among other places, sold at: Annie & Company
1325 Madison Avenue
New York
www.annieandco.com
Annie & Company deliver to Europe.

BC Garn (Denmark)
Agent in Norway: John Einarsen a/S
Hønefoss
Tel: 32 12 90 77
www.ekey.no

Cascade Yarns (USA),
see www.cascadeyarns.com

Filatura Di Crosa (Italy),
see www.filaturadicrosa.com or
www.vimar1991.com
Zara can be replaced with Sterk
from Du Store Alpakka

Lanartus (Italy)
Among other places, sold at: Husfliden Oslo.

Martha Pullen (USA)
149 Old Big Cove Road
Brownsboro, AL 35741
www.marthapullen.com

Schachenmayr (Germany)
Agent in Norway: Coats Knappehuset AS,
Ulset,
Tel: 55 53 93 00
www.coatscrafts.no

Stitch Craft Create (UK)
Brunel House,
Forde Close,
Newton Abbot,
Devon, TQ12 4PU
www.stitchcraftcreate.co.uk

INDEX

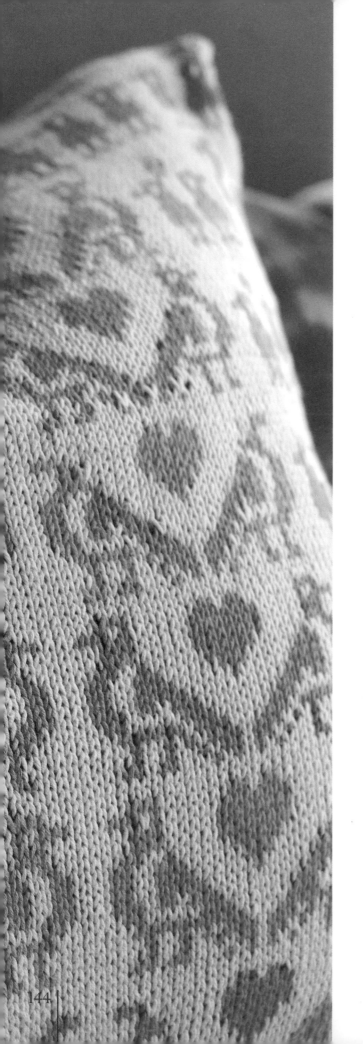

A DAVID & CHARLES BOOK
© CAPPELEN DAMM AS 2013

Originally published as Putefest by Cappelen Damm, Norway, 2012
First published in the UK and USA in 2013
by F&W Media International, Ltd

David & Charles is an imprint of F&W Media International, Ltd
Brunel House, Forde Close, Newton Abbot, TQ12 4PU, UK

F&W Media International, Ltd is a subsidiary of F+W Media, Inc
10151 Carver Road, Suite #200, Blue Ash, OH 45242, USA

ISBN-13: 978-1-4463-0425-9 paperback
ISBN-10: 1-4463-0425-6 paperback

Printed in China by RR Donnelley for
F&W Media International, Ltd
Brunel House, Forde Close, Newton Abbot, TQ12 4PU, UK

10 9 8 7 6 5 4 3 2 1

Photography: Guri Pfeifer
Stylist: Alexandra Ville France
Book design: Laila Gundersen

F+W Media publishes high quality books on a wide range of subjects.
For more great book ideas visit: **www.stitchcraftcreate.co.uk**